REBELLION,
RACISM,
AND
REPRESENTATION

THE ADAM CLAYTON POWELL CASE AND ITS ANTECEDENTS

REBELLION, RACISM, AND REPRESENTATION

THE ADAM CLAYTON POWELL CASE AND ITS ANTECEDENTS

P. A. DIONISOPOULOS

NORTHERN ILLINOIS UNIVERSITY PRESS

DEKALB, ILLINOIS

ISBN: 0–87580–018–1
LC: 76–125335
Copyright © 1970 by Northern Illinois University Press
DeKalb, Illinois 60115
All rights reserved.
Printed in the United States of America

To my parents, George and Catherine Dionisopoulos,
To my wife's parents, James and Bessie Nasios, and
To my great teachers, colleagues, and friends,
Foster H. Sherwood, H. Arthur Steiner, Currin V.
Shields, and Charles S. Hyneman

Contents

Preface

There is surprisingly little information in the literature of political science and American history about the power of each branch of Congress to judge the election, returns, and qualifications of its members. If there are any such references in books and articles on American government, politics, and more specifically to Congress, they are to the several spectacular cases involving Brigham Roberts, the polygamist, and Victor Berger, the Socialist-pacifist.

This lack of information and systematic study of the many instances in which either the House or the Senate has exercised its quasi-judicial power with respect to a member probably explains the disagreement and confusion that arose in Congress, in the press, and even within the academic community when Adam Clayton Powell was denied a seat in the House of Representatives in 1967. Indeed, disagreement both with respect to the constitutional questions and the meaning and applicability of precedents was evident even in Congress during the Powell debates. Thus there appears to be an urgent need for a thoroughgoing historical examination of all prominent cases of the past in order to gain valid explanations of the most recent cases.

As both the Adam Clayton Powell and the Julian Bond cases indicate, there are implications for more than the constituencies that elect the candidates and the need of legislators to protect the honor and dignity of their branch of Congress. Social issues, whether pertaining to civil rights, race relations, Vietnam, or democracy itself, might in the future add to the significance of this power of a legislative body to judge the "fitness" of the men elected to serve therein.

It is therefore with an eye to scholarly values, social implications, and the meaning and processes of democracy that I have undertaken research and written on this topic.

P. ALLAN DIONISOPOULOS

DeKalb, Illinois
May 1970

REBELLION,
RACISM,
AND
REPRESENTATION

THE ADAM CLAYTON POWELL CASE AND ITS ANTECEDENTS

I

Powell v. McCormack:
A Questionable Decision with Reasonable Goals

On June 16, 1969, the Supreme Court declared that the House
of Representatives had exceeded its constitutional authority in
denying membership to Adam Clayton Powell, who had served
the Eighteenth (Harlem) Congressional District in New York for
twenty-two years.[1] This was a decision of great political significance in that it repudiated a congressional practice of long
standing, revealed the Court's preference for two democratic
principles that on a number of occasions had been sacrificed on
behalf of that practice, and posed the possibility of a confrontation between the legislative and judicial branches of the national
government. If only for these reasons, *Powell* v. *McCormack*
merits more than passing attention. However, on February 2,
1970, the Supreme Court refused to hear an appeal in which
Powell requested $55,000 in back salary for 1967 and 1968,

---

[1] Powell v. McCormack, 89 S. Ct. 1944 (1969). In this first case
Representative Powell charged that the House "had excluded him uncon-
stitutionally." Although the Supreme Court decided in his favor on that
occasion, in a later case in February 1970, Powell v. Hart, the Court was
unable to provide the judicial remedy which would have made its first
decision more meaningful.

recovery of a $25,000 congressional fine imposed upon him in January 1969 (when he was seated in Congress), and reestablishment of his seniority as a twenty-two-year veteran of the House of Representatives.

The contradictions between these two decisions are much too patent to be ignored. On the one hand, in June 1969 the Court acted as though it had the answer to constitutional questions of almost two hundred years' standing. In February 1970, on the other hand, in refusing Powell the judgments he sought, the Court not only reflected its uncertainty about the constitutional issues but revealed that it did not have the power to enforce a decision that only eight months earlier it had claimed was judicially enforceable. Since these decisions have implications for both the American political system and democracy itself, it is appropriate that we determine precisely what they are and how they fit into American history.

From 1789 to 1969, each chamber had been the sole judge of whether a member-elect was qualified to serve in Congress. But now that the Supreme Court has claimed the right to review such congressional decisions, an external restraint has been imposed. Whether, in fact, a new principle has been introduced depends upon several factors. There is every likelihood, given the long history during which each chamber has served as sole judge of such matters, given the principle of separation of powers, and given the failure of the Court to follow through by enforcing its own decision, that no change in practice will have been made. It is also possible that *Powell* v. *McCormack* means something less than has been claimed for it.

To underscore the latter point, we may note that the first decision seemed to remove a contradiction that had long existed —a practice that seemingly had been sanctioned both by the Constitution and by precedents but was nevertheless contrary to two democratic principles. The first principle is that power must be subject to restraints so that it will not be used arbitrarily and capriciously. The second principle, which is closely related, is the right of the people to be represented by men of their own choosing. Most likely some kind of qualification requirements are needed, but they should be minimal, standardized, and uniformly applied. Otherwise there is the possibility that arbitrariness and caprice will enter into decisions about the qualifications of a member-elect.

Having acknowledged that the Court attacked this contradiction in *Powell* v. *McCormack,* we must determine whether Representative Powell—and others—had sound reasons for acclaiming this decision; and the decision of February 1970 (in *Powell* v. *Hart*) is one reason for doubting the durability and viability of *Powell* v. *McCormack.* In proceeding with this inquiry it also is necessary that we consider how and why the contradiction emerged, whether there were any constitutional or other justifications for the legislative chambers' acting as they had so often on occasions prior to Powell's being denied membership, and the strengths and weaknesses of *Powell* v. *McCormack.* Thus the major points of inquiry can be identified in this chapter, but their elaboration is possible only if we explore the historical record from the Constitutional Convention in 1787 to the House's refusal to give the oath of office to Powell in 1967. We must therefore begin by noting the source of the contradiction.

Article I, section 5 of the Constitution empowers each chamber of Congress to be "the judge of the elections, returns and qualifications of its own members" and to "punish its members for disorderly behaviour," which includes expulsion. The only limitation on these quasi-judicial powers is that a member may be expelled only "with the concurrence of two thirds." Since there are not in this or any other section of the Constitution other specified limitations on the *exercise* of these powers, their exact scope and nature were at all times in doubt. This point can best be understood by noting some of the questions that had plagued members of Congress on a number of earlier occasions and that also were present in the Powell matter.

In the nineteenth and twentieth centuries, each house had been confronted with two fundamental constitutional questions. First, may the House or Senate devise its own test of fitness, as the occasion demands, in deciding whether a member-elect is eligible to serve in Congress? Second, in exercising either the power to judge qualifications or to punish a member for misconduct are the legislative bodies subject only to self-imposed restraints, or may their decisions be overturned either in the courts or at the polls? Because of the inexplicit language of the Constitution, answers to these questions could not be readily obtained by reference to that document. In time, therefore, each chamber produced its own answers. Moreover, neither chamber had been subjected to other than self-imposed restraints before the Powell decision in 1969.

Beyond these fundamental questions still others arise—for example, questions about time and place. Must a member-elect meet the qualification requirements the moment he is elected, or by the time he presents himself to receive the oath of office? And at what time and place must an offense have been committed for a chamber to take jurisdiction over a case and exercise its power to punish a member? May the House or Senate punish a member for misconduct even though an offense was committed before his election or reelection? May it take jurisdiction if the offensive act was committed beyond the halls of Congress and even outside the District of Columbia? Thus the relevancy of time and place questions to the Powell case and the reason why authoritative answers must be provided.

The inexact language of the Constitution made it possible for each chamber to define the dimensions of these quasi-judicial powers and to exercise its powers in arbitrary fashion. This situation, however, had become untenable—as Justice Douglas contended—because each house was in a position to decide whether a member-elect's *beliefs* were acceptable, and could deny the oath of office to a man by reason of his race. The need to restrain this power was made even more urgent by the requirements of democracy. As Justice Douglas observed:

At root, however, is the basic integrity of the electoral process. Today we proclaim the constitutional principle of "one man one vote." When that principle is followed and the electors chose a person who is repulsive to the Establishment in Congress, by what constitutional authority can that group of electors be disenfranchised?[2]

Douglas saw the problem as a basic conflict between a practice of long standing and the need to safeguard a democratic principle; and this, we believe, is the essence of the problem. Accordingly, and in keeping with constitutionally sanctioned practices

---

[2] Concurring opinion in Powell v. McCormack, 89 S. Ct. 1944, 1980 (1969).

of more than a hundred years' standing, Powell was not the only member-elect who has been denied office on the ground that he did not meet the standards prescribed by the House or Senate. And on each occasion, of course, the voters within the relevant constituencies had been denied the right of representation by a man who passed the minimal standards but not the arbitrarily imposed fitness tests.

In view of these facts, *Powell* v. *McCormack* assumes special importance because it defined the dimensions of congressional power and served as a vehicle for reaching democratic goals.

Does the First *Powell* Decision Provide Answers?

Despite the apparent accomplishments of *Powell* v. *McCormack*, we must be skeptical for various reasons. For example, how effectively did the Court answer the several pertinent constitutional questions? Specifically, may each chamber specify its own standards, and may Congress use its legislative power to prescribe still other qualifications? By taking jurisdiction over this case and rendering an opinion favorable to Powell, the Court not only repudiated the claim that this is an exclusive power but identified the qualifications that may be considered. For the first time in 180 years, the power of each chamber had been subjected to an external restraint. In exercising this power to render its own verdicts, the Court also said, the chambers may consider only whether a member-elect meets the age, citizenship, and inhabitancy requirements of the Constitution. As long as a member-elect meets the requirements of age (at least twenty-five for a representative and thirty for a senator), citizenship (seven and nine years respectively), and inhabitancy (members-elect must reside in the state from which they are elected to Congress), he is eligible for membership. Therefore in denying the oath of office to Representative-elect Powell in 1967 the House had exceeded its constitutional power.

The trouble with this conclusion, however, is that eight, not three, qualifications and/or disqualifications are stipulated in the Constitution. The five criteria in addition to age, citizenship, and inhabitancy will be identified at this point and their significance noted in the next chapter.

The first of these five criteria is found in Article I, section 3. Any person who is convicted in an impeachment proceeding is disqualified for all offices "of honor, trust, or profit under the United States."

A second disqualification is defined in Article I, section 6: "No person holding any office under the United States shall be a member of either house during his continuance in office."

Both the guaranty clause of Article IV, section 4 and the decision of the Supreme Court in *Luther* v. *Borden* (1849)[3] identify a third disqualification. The clause guarantees "to every State in the Union a republican form of government," and it is the reason for this statement of the Court in the *Luther* case: "When the Senators or Representatives of a State are admitted into the councils of the Union, the authority of the government under which they are appointed, as well as its republican charac-ter, is recognized by the proper constitutional authority." By the same token, if a state does not have a republican form of govern-ment, the House and Senate may refuse to seat its members-elect. In such event the constitutional qualifications of age, citizenship, and inhabitancy would not be the governing criteria.

A fourth provision requires that all national and state officials "be bound by oath or affirmation to support this Constitution."[4]

The fifth disqualification was added in 1868 with the adoption of the Fourteenth Amendment:

No person shall be a Senator or Representative . . . who, having previously taken an oath . . . to support the Constitution of the United States, shall have engaged in insurrection or rebellion against the same, or given aid or comfort to the enemies thereof.

In a footnote to the *Powell* decision the Court acknowledged these other constitutional disqualifications; however, in the body of its opinion it identified only age, citizenship, and inhabitancy. By implying in the text that there are only three and acknowledg-ing in a footnote that there are eight criteria, the Court created an unfortunate contradiction that can only detract from the

---

[3] 47 U.S. (7 How.) 1.
[4] Article VI, clause 3.

decision and raise doubts about the substance of *Powell* v. *McCormack*.[5]

If the Court's answer to the qualification question is clouded by the doubt created by this contradiction, its answer to the time and place question is even more murky. The several questions we have noted relating to time and place were very much present in the *Powell* case and therefore must be discussed.

When exercising its power to judge the conduct of a member, may the House or Senate consider allegations of wrongdoing during a previous Congress? This was precisely the question in *Powell*. The charges of misconduct against Powell in 1967 were that he was guilty of wrongdoing while previously a member of Congress. The place factor was also introduced in that one of the reasons for considering him unfit to serve in Congress was the fact that he was in contempt of the courts of New York.

The members of Congress saw different courses of action open to them. Some, such as the members of the Select Committee that investigated the allegations of misconduct, recommended that he be seated but that a $40,000 fine be imposed upon him. Others believed that Powell should be seated and that the House then act to expel him. Those who prevailed advocated a third course: exclusion.

Although these several courses of action were dictated by different interpretations of the Constitution, they reflected a common belief that the House could act. The allegations were about wrongdoing before Powell's reelection in November 1966, and they included his being declared in contempt of New York courts. Therefore each of these three groups of representatives, in advocating its course of action, had no doubt that the power of the chamber extended to matters arising in the past and elsewhere. The same belief was shared by a majority in the House in 1969;

---

[5] The Court stated that "in judging qualifications of its members Congress is limited to the standing qualifications prescribed in the Constitution" (89 S. Ct. 1944, 1979 [1969]). Having identified only the three qualifications in its text, the Court thus implies that age, citizenship, and inhabitancy are "standing qualifications." Yet in a footnote it acknowledged that there are eight in all. See "A Commentary on the Constitutional Issues in the Powell and Related Cases," 17 *Journal of Public Law* 103, 111–115 (1968), cited by the Court at 89 S. Ct. 1944, 1963, fn. 41 (1969).

when Powell was seated in January 1969, a $25,000 fine was imposed upon him. Since these facts suggest the breadth and significance of the time and place factors, we should consider how the Court looked upon this aspect of congressional power.

Only by implication is there even the hint of an answer. After acknowledging that "Congress has an interest in preserving its institutional integrity," Chief Justice Warren declared:

That interest can be sufficiently safeguarded by the exercise of its power to punish its members for disorderly behavior and, in extreme cases, to expel a member with the concurrence of two-thirds.[6]

This statement was made in conjunction with another in which the Court denied the House the power to exclude a member-elect unless he failed to meet the standing qualifications of the Constitution.

For two reasons it is permissible to label this a murky answer, if indeed it is any answer at all. First, the Court was underscoring its point that neither chamber may use the power to exclude (which requires only a majority vote) as a means for subverting the constitutional requirement of a two-thirds vote in order to expel. Since a majority vote can be more easily obtained than two-thirds, the Court seemed to impose a reasonable requirement and one that is in accord with the Constitution. But—setting aside the distinction between exclusion and expulsion—had the Court thereby invited each chamber to protect its institutional integrity by seating a member-elect and then expelling him because of past acts of misconduct?

Since more than two-thirds voted to exclude Powell (307 to 116), it is likely that he could have been given the oath of office and then expelled. However that would not have provided a more definitive answer as to the time factor in relation to the power to expel, or indeed to the power of the House to impose the fine of $25,000. In this respect *Powell* v. *McCormack* was not a significant victory for either an external restraint or for the people of Harlem who elected Powell to be their representative in Congress.

The second reason is found not so much in what Warren described as the proper interest of each chamber in protecting its institutional integrity as in what this had meant on other occa-

---

[6] Powell v. McCormack, 89 S. Ct. 1944, 1978 (1969).

sions—instances in which a legislative chamber contended it had to have an exclusive voice on such matters to guarantee that its institutional integrity would be protected. To develop this line of our discussion, we will cite arguments from as long ago as 1807 and as recently as 1967.

Both matters, exclusive power and institutional integrity, were advanced in 1807 by Senators Buckner Thruston and John Quincy Adams in the case of Senator John Smith of Ohio, who had been indicted by a federal grand jury as a co-conspirator of Aaron Burr. However, when the case against Burr was thrown out of court by John Marshall, the Jefferson administration decided not to prosecute Smith. Nevertheless, President Jefferson sent the Senate a copy of the indictment and other documents dealing with Smith's alleged conspiracy with Burr. Apparently Jefferson wanted the Senate to punish Smith, even though he could not be prosecuted in the regular courts of law. This posed a serious question, which was answered in the statements of Thruston and Adams.

The Senate, Thruston declared, has an "unlimited power to expel a member" even though the offenses of which he is charged "are not criminal in nature."[7] He also described the Senate as both accuser and judge in such cases.

His statement made claims of a broad nature. First, a legislative chamber has an exclusive voice in these matters. Second, the chamber not only plays all the roles in determining whether a member is guilty as charged but may even act in a way that is denied to a court of law. This second point was of special importance to legislators who, in the Smith and other cases, claimed that institutional integrity could be protected only if their jurisdiction was exclusive.

Adams, who served as chairman of a special committee that investigated the charges against Smith, lent additional support to Thruston's claims. Speaking for his committee, Adams advised the Senate not to be deterred by the constitutional deficiency of the charges against Smith:

When the darling of the people's choice has become their deadliest foe, can it enter the imagination of a reasonable man that the sanctu-

---

[7] *Debates and Proceedings of the U.S. Congress,* 10th Congress, 1st sess., p. 42 (1807), reel no. 4 (Ann Arbor: University Microfilms, 1955).

ary of their legislature must remain polluted with his presence, until a court of common law, with its pace of a snail, can ascertain whether his crime was committed on the right or on the left bank of a river?[8]

Members of the committee were convinced, Adams said, "that the dereliction of the prosecution . . . cannot, in the slightest degree, remove the imputation which the accusations of the grand jury have brought to the door of Mr. Smith."[9]

Neither "the darling of the people's choice" nor the fact that the indictment was no more than a suspicion of guilt and no prosecution was possible were to stand in the way of the Senate. It had to have ample power to assure itself of not being "polluted with his presence." The vitality and acceptability of Thruston's and Adams's arguments are reflected in the vote to expel Smith which fell just one vote short of the necessary two-thirds (19 to 10). Indeed, so convincing was this vote against him that Smith immediately tendered a letter of resignation.[10]

As has been shown in recent cases involving black militants, such notions are not confined to the past. Julian Bond's statements against the war in Vietnam and the draft caused difficulty for him when he presented his credentials to the Georgia House of Representatives. The latter denied Bond membership, declaring that his comments "are reprehensible and are such as tend to bring discredit to and disrespect of the House."[11] And when Powell initiated his suit against members of the United States House of Representatives, Minority Leader Ford argued:

If this body is the judge in these matters, there cannot be any other judge nor any higher appeal . . . [The Powell] judgment is, in my view, final, unless it is changed in the future by the House of Representatives. Neither the Senate, within the legislative branch, nor any court created by the Constitution or by Congress in the judicial branch, nor any officer of the executive branch, has any jurisdiction here.[12]

---

[8] "Report on Senator John Smith," 3 *Writings of John Quincy Adams, 1801–1810* 183 (1914).

[9] Ibid.

[10] *Debates and Proceedings of the U.S. Congress*, 10th Congress, 1st sess., pp. 324–331 (1808), reel no. 4 (Ann Arbor: University Microfilms, 1955).

[11] Quoted by the Supreme Court in Bond v. Floyd, 385 U.S. 116, 125 (1966).

[12] 113 *Congressional Record* H. 2400, daily ed. (Mar. 9, 1967).

Representative Ford might have added that the voters within a member-elect's constituency are also denied a voice on such a matter.

The foregoing claims, made at different periods in time, illustrate the attitudes of members of Congress with respect to the two points about the power to judge residing exclusively with each chamber and the need to protect institutional integrity. When we add to these still another matter, the principle of separation of powers, we get a better idea of why it is necessary to raise a procedural doubt about *Powell* v. *McCormack*.

"Through a Political Thicket into Political Quicksand"

In refusing to enter a judgment in favor of Adam Clayton Powell, a federal district court judge, George L. Hart, Jr., said that for him to order the House, its members, or employees to perform in a certain way on the issue of membership "would be for the court to crash through a political thicket into political quicksand."[13] The meaning of this statement is clear. The principle of separation of powers operates in such a way as to vest some matters exclusively in one branch of government, and to cross the boundaries created by this principle is to invite a confrontation between two branches. Obviously, Judge Hart was not anxious to breach the principle and face the possibility that the House would hurl his decision back at him rather than obey it. Although in the later rejection of Powell's second appeal (in *Powell* v. *Hart*) the Supreme Court did not render a written opinion, its reasons for turning Powell down at least appeared to be quite similar.

The Supreme Court had not been timid in June 1969, but an act of courage could not in itself overcome the reluctance of Congress to obey the federal judges. Nor was it likely that Congress would have been forced to withdraw from the field. If the Court had merely stated a new constitutional doctrine and invited Congress to adopt it, that would have been one thing. To state a new constitutional doctrine and announce that it can be enforced is something else. Because the Court initially chose the latter course, albeit with a conciliatory gesture in observance of

---

[13] Powell v. McCormack, 266 F. Supp. 354, 359 (1967).

the principle of separation of powers, let us determine how the Court saw its own role and how it saw its decision as being enforceable. We may then consider how these views were implicitly rejected by the Court in *Powell* v. *Hart* (1970), thus restoring the situation that prevailed before June 1969.

There had been tacit acknowledgment of the principle of separation of powers in *Powell* v. *McCormack*. Chief Justice Warren had declared: "Although this action should be dismissed against respondent Congressmen [Representatives McCormack, Albert, Ford, et al.], it may be sustained against their agents."[14] But if the members of a coordinate branch of government may not be held answerable in the courts for their actions, of what consequence is a judgment against their employees? Warren found the answer to this question in a nineteenth-century case, *Kilbourn* v. *Thompson* (1880).[15] On that occasion Kilbourn had received $20,000 for false arrest from Thompson, the sergeant at arms, who had acted under orders from the House. Payment of the judgment had indeed been made; however it was paid by Congress, not by Thompson.[16] This meant, then, that the House had accepted the Supreme Court's declaration that the powers of Congress to investigate and to compel the appearance of and testimony by witnesses are subject to limitations. Had Congress refused to appropriate the money, Kilbourn could have done little by way of further judicial action.

Kilbourn does not appear to be as workable a precedent as the Court declared. Given the much different circumstances in the *Powell* case, it was doubtful, even before *Powell* v. *Hart*, that *Kilbourn* was a precedent at all. The House had not authorized a payment of $80,000 to Powell (his back salary for 1967 and 1968 and the fine imposed in 1969) and the restoration of his seniority. There was, then, no way the Court could have punished such agents of the House as the paymaster and the clerk. On the other hand, had the House accepted a judgment by the federal courts and made restitution, as well as restored Powell's senior-

---

[14] 89 S. Ct. 1944, 1979 (1969).

[15] 103 U.S. 168. The Court's use of Kilbourn as a governing precedent is found at 89 S. Ct. 1944, 1954 (1969).

[16] 16 *Congressional Record* 1056 (1885). This money and the court costs incurred by Thompson were included in the sundry civil appropriations bill.

ity, this would have been a consequence of its acknowledging the wisdom of a judicial pronouncement rather than fear that its employees would be punished by the courts.

In dismissing the suit against elected members of the House, the Court had impliedly acknowledged the impossibility of compelling them to act. Simultaneously, by holding that an action against House employees may be sustained the Court rendered an unenforceable judgment. Political reality demands that we acknowledge the only way *Powell* v. *McCormack* could have been made operational: each chamber would have had to agree to reject precedents and indicate that it is preferable to honor democratic principles rather than time-sanctioned practices.

A Doubt about the Court's Historical Techniques

For purposes of this study, precedents are highly important and must be examined. In part the justification for inquiring into precedents is their revelation of the way in which each chamber came to define the dimensions of its power and how "the law" had evolved on a case-by-case basis. This inquiry is also justified by what must be described as the substantive deficiencies of the Court's opinion in *Powell* v. *McCormack*.

A case such as Powell's permits us to ask a hypothetical but fundamental question in a realistic context: Can the Constitution of the United States be accommodated to a new democratic principle or goal? If time-honored practices contradict democratic principles, it might appear that an accommodation cannot be reached unless the historical record underlying those practices is redefined. It would appear, given the foregoing charge about the substantive weaknesses of *Powell*, that the Court believed an accommodation was possible only if the historical record could be distorted. As is shown by the desegregation decision, *Brown* v. *Board of Education* (1954),[17] the historical record can be forthrightly acknowledged at the same time the Constitution is accommodated to new democratic practices.

In 1954 the Court was intent upon promoting a democratic doctrine, human equality, by subverting a constitutionally sanctioned practice of more than fifty years' standing: separate but

---

[17] 347 U.S. 483.

equal school facilities for whites and blacks. The new goal could not have been reached either by rewriting or distorting the historical record that surrounded the adoption of the Fourteenth Amendment in 1868. At the time this amendment entered into force, a number of Northern states and the District of Columbia had segregated school systems, a fact acknowledged by Chief Justice Warren in the *Brown* decision when he said:

> In approaching this problem, we cannot turn the clock back to 1868 when the Fourteenth Amendment was adopted, or even to 1896 when *Plessy* v. *Ferguson* was written. We must consider public education in the light of its full development and its present place in American life throughout the nation.[18]

For part of its consideration of the "present place" of public education the Court relied upon findings by social scientists, upon studies that disclosed that separate educational facilities created a sense of inferiority within black children. Thus these findings underscored the fact that the doctrine of separate but equal facilities resulted in superior and inferior racial classifications and thereby did violence to the democratic doctrine of human equality. Consequently the Court directly assaulted the constitutionally sanctioned practice to which it had given its blessing more than fifty years earlier.

The important lesson here is that the Court did not have to revise history by judicial fiat to bring the Constitution into line with an important democratic doctrine. Rather than redefine the historical context within which the Fourteenth Amendment was adopted, the Supreme Court forthrightly rejected the practice that was found to be contrary to democratic theory. Having successfully used this direct approach in one instance, there is no reason why on other occasions the Court must view a new democratic goal as attainable only by rewriting history.

This chapter has offered only two pieces of evidence—the contradiction between the decision's text and footnote and the inadequate portrayal of the situation in *Kilbourn* v. *Thompson* (1880)—in raising a doubt about the substance of the *Powell* decision. Since the whole story cannot be told in this chapter, it is necessary to state a thesis and in subsequent chapters develop supporting evidence for it: the Court's decision in *Powell* v.

---

[18] Ibid., p. 492.

McCormack lacks a sound historical foundation and is made deficient thereby. In later chapters we will determine whether this thesis is valid by inquiring into the same historical record that was available to the Court. For the moment, however, it will suffice to present justifications for entertaining doubts about the historical record's conclusions in *Powell.*

At the outset we should note that there is nothing unique about scholars' subjecting judicial decisions to critical analysis and that members of the Court often disagree about the historical record. Constitutional scholars would therefore be remiss were they to accept without question every decision handed down. Moreover, we must note that the Court's historical techniques have been deplored by prominent constitutional scholars on various occasions.[19] In line with the tradition of critical analysis, Professor Kelly has even characterized the Court as presenting an "extended essay in constitutional history of the ['law office'] variety."[20] Whether *Powell* should be similarly characterized can be determined only after examination of the complete historical record, from the Constitutional Convention in 1787 to the House's exclusion of Adam Clayton Powell in 1967.

A single illustration at this point will indicate the probability that *Powell* v. *McCormack* is indeed an "extended essay in constitutional history of the 'law office' variety." Both the majority opinion by Warren and Douglas's concurring opinion refer to a statement by a nineteenth-century constitutional lawyer and member of the Supreme Court, Joseph Story,[21] and indicate that the Court had previously accepted arguments that were advanced in briefs for Powell.[22] These references allege that Story rejected the claim that Congress may add to the list of constitutional qualifications. In fact, however, Justice Story did not even mention Congress. The purported claim was supposedly found in

---

[19] Such as Professor A. H. Kelly in his "CLIO and the Court: An Illicit Love Affair," *1965, The Supreme Court Review* 119 (1965).

[20] Ibid., p. 122. By "law office variety" Kelly means that only supportive data are selected; contradictory data are ignored and other relevant evidence is not evaluated.

[21] For these references see 89 S. Ct. 1944; 1972, n. 69; and 1980, n. 2 (1969).

[22] Powell's brief is found at *In re Adam Clayton Powell: Hearings before Select Committee pursuant to H. Res. 1,* 90th Congress, 1st sess. 7 (1967). Another brief, by the American Civil Liberties Union, was printed in 113 Congressional Record H. 1376, n. 5, daily ed. (1967).

section 625 of Story's *Commentaries on the Constitution*, but sections 624 through 629 are directed solely to the question whether the *states* may add to the list of qualifications. And Story argued that the *states* may not prescribe additional qualifications for members of Congress.[23] Garbled or misinterpreted citations may surely be classified as essays of the "law office variety."

Still another reason for doubting the historical veracity of the conclusion reached in *Powell* v. *McCormack* is the failure of the Court to consider the precedents of the House and Senate and "the law" as it had evolved on a case-by-case basis. In part this inadequacy in the Court's decision can be attributed to its reliance on Hind's *Precedents* or other official publications that present too scanty a picture of the issues involved in earlier cases and the decisions reached by the House or Senate. This inadequate understanding of previous cases led Justice Douglas to say: "A man is not seated because he is a Socialist or a Communist." Then he referred to the case of Victor Berger and cited Cannon's *Precedents of the House of Representatives of the United States.*

While it is true that Berger was Socialist, the House did not refuse to seat him in 1919 and 1920 because of his ideological commitment. As a pacifist, however, he had been critical of America's entry into World War I; indeed, he had been convicted under the Espionage Act of 1917 because of various statements he had made. In denying him membership the House had decided he was ineligible by reason of a disqualification in section 3 of the Fourteenth Amendment, where it is stated:

No person shall be a Senator or Representative in Congress . . . who, having previously taken an oath, as a member of Congress . . . to support the Constitution of the United States, shall have . . . given aid or comfort to the enemies thereof.

Because Berger took this oath in 1911, when he was first elected to Congress as a Socialist, the question for the House was whether he had later violated it. In speaking against America's involvement in World War I, had Berger, an Austrian-born and naturalized American, given aid or comfort to the Central Powers? That his party identification had nothing to do with this question is shown in the fact that he was seated as a representative

---

[23] 1 *Story's Commentaries on the Constitution* sec. 624–629 (1873).

in 1911 and again in 1923—both before and after he was denied membership. Thus the facts in the Berger case are scarcely in line with Douglas's statement.[24]

Rather than rely upon Hind's or Cannon's *Precedents* or the record in the *Powell* decision for an explanation of how "the law" evolved, we will proceed independently and explore all the landmark cases of the past. And in undertaking such an inquiry we must be aware of four things. First, although on occasion a chamber may have claimed it could not judge a member-elect except for age, citizenship, or inhabitancy, the mere act of judging such a case had important consequences. Second, such cases were not always limited to a single issue, and multiple questions became so intermingled that no single, clear-cut decision emerged. Third, while our attention will focus primarily on the constitutional question about the qualifications of members-elect, we will see that the power to determine eligibility assumed a relationship to other powers, such as punishment for misconduct either by censure or expulsion. Finally, we must be aware of the importance of precedents in American constitutional history. The flexibility of the Constitution is not a consequence of the formal amending process but of informal means of change. Precedents have contributed so importantly to other developments under the Constitution, and are so illustrative of how changes are accomplished through informal means, that we are hardly in a position to condemn their use in this area.

Since the Supreme Court did not explain why it rejected Powell's appeal to recover back pay, the fine, and his seniority, we can only speculate on its reasons, such as the operability of the principle of separation of powers and the nonenforceability of the first *Powell* decision.

Important though these reasons are, they do not compare with

---

[24] See his concurring opinion at 89 S. Ct. 1944, 1980 (1969). The same historical inaccuracy is present in his statement: "Another is not seated because in his district members of a minority are systematically excluded from voting." In making this statement he also cited 6 Cannon, *Precedents of the House of Representatives of the United States*, sec. 122 (1935). The fact is that such a practice is condoned by the Fourteenth Amendment: "But when the right to vote at any election . . . is denied to any of the male inhabitants of such State . . . the basis of representation in Congress shall be reduced" (sec. 2). During Reconstruction, denial of membership was also based on a state's not having a republican form of government, as guaranteed by Article IV of the Constitution.

what is even more significant for the American people. What we have, in fact, is a return to the earlier practice of each chamber. Thus each house of Congress may again devise its own standards for judging members-elect, exercising a power that is limited only by self-restraint and, because of its arbitrary character, subversive of the right of the people to choose the men who will represent them in Congress.

In this chapter doubts were expressed about the historic verifiability and the enforceability of the Court's first decision in *Powell* v. *McCormack*. The fact that the Court could not enforce that decision in *Powell* v. *Hart* in February 1970 lends support to our skepticism about the breadth of judicial power in such a case. The other reason for questioning *Powell* v. *McCormack*— doubts as to its historic verifiability—could not be adequately discussed in this chapter. We must, therefore, examine the same historical record that was available to the Supreme Court and come to our own conclusions.

II

Inquiry into the Constitutional Questions

We have claimed that *Powell* v. *McCormack* may be criticized for substantive reasons, that it lacked a sound historical basis. That only part of the historical record was explored by the majority in arriving at its decision, that the House exceeded its authority in denying membership to Powell. And that the *Powell* decision turned upon an oversimplified interpretation of the Constitution and the historical record. In fact, however, such simple interpretations are not permissible because more important matters must be considered, which will be brought out in this chapter.

In proceeding with our argument it is necessary to contradict various claims in *The Making of the Constitution*, whose author, Professor Charles Warren, has often been cited as an authority on constitutional issues.[1] His examination of the proceedings of

The material in this chapter was adapted from P. A. Dionisopoulos, "A Commentary on the Constitutional Issues in the Powell and Related Cases," 17 *Journal of Public Law* 103 (1968).

[1] For example, see Powell v. McCormack, 89 S. Ct. 1944, 1969 (1969); Powell and ACLU briefs, *In re Adam Clayton Powell: Hearings before Select Committee pursuant to H. Res. 1*, 90th Congress, 1st sess., pp. 13, 29 (1967); and Chief Justice Warren's opinion in Bond v. Floyd, 87 S. Ct. 339, 349, fn. 13 (1966).

the Constitutional Convention led him to the conclusion that neither house of Congress had been granted

the right to establish any qualifications for its members, other than those qualifications established by the Constitution itself, viz., age, citizenship, and residence. For certainly it did not intend that a single branch of Congress should possess a power which the Convention had expressly refused to vest in the whole Congress.[2]

Two points in his statement should be kept in mind as we explore the constitutional issues. First, there are only three (not eight) grounds upon which the House or Senate may judge its members-elect: age, citizenship, and inhabitancy. Second, not only is one chamber, acting independently, prohibited from adding to this list, but both houses collectively are denied authority to use their legislative powers to prescribe additional qualifications. By reconstructing a portion of the 1787 convention's proceedings we can see why Professor Warren came to these conclusions. However, it is necessary to go beyond them to three other matters, all of which undermine his thesis.

The Issues at the Constitutional Convention

Relatively few days were devoted by the delegates at the Constitutional Convention of 1787 to discussions about the qualifications for members of Congress. The Randolph (Virginia) plan of government referred to just two criteria: age and a prohibition against holding another office, national or state. Although Randolph's statement of principles did not stipulate the mimimum ages the convention agreed with little controversy on twenty-five years for representatives and thirty for senators. The delegates also agreed in part to Randolph's recommendation that congressmen (i.e., members of both the House and the Senate) should not simultaneously hold another national office, but some disagreement with respect to the office-holding prohibition appeared later in the convention's deliberations. However, by July 26, 1787, when much of the groundwork had been completed and the Committee on Detail began preparing a draft, the resolutions that had been agreed upon reflected the will of the majority.

---

[2] Warren, Charles, *The Making of the Constitution* (New York: Barnes & Noble, 1937), p. 421.

Besides the resolutions on minimum ages and against holding other offices, the convention issued an instruction to the Committee on Detail

to receive a clause or clauses, requiring certain qualifications of property and citizenship, in the United States, for the executive, the judiciary, and the members of both branches of the legislature of the United States.[3]

Such a resolution had been produced just prior to the committee's commencing work on the draft of a constitution, and only at that time were the matters of citizenship, property, and unsettled accounts introduced into the deliberations. Colonel Mason of Virginia proposed "landed property and citizenship" as qualifications and that persons who have unsettled accounts with or are indebted to the United States be ineligible for national office. While his proposals had the support of some, they were criticized by others. A requirement of landownership, some critics argued, discriminated against those who invested their funds in commercial enterprises, and the proposal regarding unsettled accounts was objected to as cruel and unjust to many patriots who had served in various ways during the Revolutionary War and were still awaiting a settlement of accounts.

George Mason and Pierce Butler (who was born in Ireland) were among the delegates who expressed concern about admitting naturalized citizens to public office. Fearful that foreign governments might influence American policies by means of naturalized citizens, these delegates demanded a lengthy period between the date of naturalization and the time at which foreign-born citizens would be qualified for national office. At least with respect to the requirement that only "natural-born" Americans be eligible for the presidency and vice presidency, this concern about foreign influence was general. But with respect to citizenship or naturalization qualifications for members of Congress, the delegates agreed to relatively short periods of time: seven years for representatives and nine years for senators.

Significantly, the delegates' opposition to Mason's property-qualification proposal was not limited to discrimination between

---

[3] *Documents Illustrative of the Formation of the Union of the American States,* House Doc. No. 398, 69th Congress, 1st sess. (Washington: GPO, 1927), p. 470 (hereafter cited as *Madison's Journal*).

land and other forms of property ownership; some delegates objected to any kind of property requirement since, in their estimation, to venerate wealth was to deny republican principles. The uniqueness of this argument in that day is seen in several states' imposition of a property test as a condition both for voters and for persons standing as candidates for public office. Ultimately, all proposals requiring property ownership as a qualification were defeated and therefore require no further comment. However, of all the proposals regarding qualifications for congressmen, those pertaining to property set the framework for our question: Did the Constitutional Convention empower the houses of Congress, either separately or jointly, to add to the list of qualifications?

On July 26, as we have noted, the convention instructed the Committee on Detail to consider "requiring certain qualifications of property and citizenship" for members of the legislative, executive, and judicial branches of the national government. But because the committee was unable to agree upon a proper formula, it postponed the matter and proposed that Congress be empowered "to establish such qualifications of the members of each House, with regard to property," as seemed expedient.[4] In the ensuing discussions and proceedings, statements by James Madison and two votes by the delegates provide a foundation for Professor Warren's thesis. Madison warned against vesting such an "improper and dangerous power in the legislature." Regarding the qualifications of both electors and elected as republican principles that "ought to be fixed by the Constitution," he suggested that the convention consider how Parliament had, on occasion, abused its power to specify qualifications.[5]

The votes on two propositions, however, are even more central to Warren's conclusions than the views of one man, notwithstanding his being the "Father of the Constitution." The first vote arose from a proposal by Gouverneur Morris, who had moved that the committee's proposal be amended by striking out the phrase "with regard to property." If adopted, the amended clause would have read:

---

[4] *Madison's Journal*, p. 473.
[5] Ibid., pp. 513–514.

The Legislature of the United States shall have authority to establish such uniform qualifications of the members of each House as to the said Legislature shall seem expedient.

By a vote of six states to three, the Morris amendment was defeated; and immediately thereafter the convention also voted down the original article proposed by the committee. Since each proposition was intended to authorize Congress to prescribe qualifications by statute, the defeat of each is proof to Professor Warren (and others) that the House and the Senate, either singly or collectively, do not have the power to prescribe additional qualifications.[6]

There can be little doubt that the majority was guided by the notion that a republic does not venerate wealth and that many delegates heeded Madison's warning of Parliament's abuse of its power to specify qualifications as "a lesson worthy of our attention." Juxtaposing Madison's warning with the committee's proposal and the convention's voting down both the proposal and the Morris amendment, Professor Warren could conclude that, by the explicit prescription of qualifications and the specific denial to Congress of the power to establish qualifications in general, "the maxim *expressio unius exclusio alterious* would seem to apply."[7]

A similar position has often been stated in congressional debates. For example, at the outset of debate in the Powell case Representative Celler said:

The Constitution lays down three qualifications for one to enter Congress—age, inhabitancy, citizenship. Mr. Powell satisfies all three. The House cannot add to these qualifications. If so, it could add, for example, a religious test or conceivably deny seats to a minority by mere majority vote.[8]

---

[6] Examples of such claims are found in the Powell and ACLU briefs, in *In re Adam Clayton Powell: Hearings before Select Committee pursuant to H. Res. 1*, pp. 13, 29; and in Chief Justice Warren's opinion in Bond v. Floyd, 87 S. Ct. 339, 349, fn. 13 (1966), and in Powell v. McCormack, 89 S. Ct. 1944, 1970 (1969).

[7] Op. cit., p. 421.

[8] *Congressional Record* H. 1920 (1967). Celler's warning about a religious test is without foundation in view of Article VI, clause 3 of the Constitution.

Since similar arguments have been voiced on other occasions,[9] it is imperative that we consider such evidence as might validate or repudiate these contentions—and three matters that undermine or at least make less certain the contentions of Professor Warren, Chief Justice Warren, Emmanuel Celler, and the authors of the Powell and the ACLU briefs. First, the Constitution contains eight, not three, qualifications. Second, the prohibition in Article VI, clause 3 of a religious qualification poses several questions. And third, a legislative enactment of the First Congress in 1790 raises a doubt especially about the validity of Professor Warren's argument.

The Number of Constitutional Qualifications

Those who argue that Congress is without authority to add to the enumerated qualifications almost inevitably refer to the three qualifications of age, citizenship, and inhabitancy rather than to the five disqualifications. Yet Article I, section 3 disqualifies any person who has been convicted in an impeachment proceeding. This disqualification applies not just to membership in Congress but to all offices "of honor, trust, or profit under the United States."

A second disqualification, and one occasionally noted in congressional debates, is found in Article I, section 6, which states that members of Congress may not hold any other office "under the United States." This provision was considered necessary to prevent undue influence by the President in legislative proceedings. Thus early in its history Congress was sufficiently jealous of its prerogatives to remove—in the words of Randolph of Virginia —"even the shadow of Executive influence"; and the lengths to which it was willing to go to preclude encroachment are demonstrated by the John P. Van Ness case of 1802.

Because Van Ness had earlier accepted a commission as major in the militia of the District of Columbia, an investigation was initiated on December 27, 1802, to determine whether he had thereby forfeited his right to membership in the House. Although

---

[9] For example, Berger's statement, 58 *Congressional Record* 8712 (1919); Senator Overton's claim, 93 ibid. 17 (1947); and the arguments of Representatives Multer and Ashley, 113 ibid. H. 10 and H. 1947 (1967).

his colleagues affirmed that Van Ness had received no compensation as an officer in the militia, and although he could have exerted little influence in behalf of the executive branch, the House was so concerned that this might serve as a dangerous precedent that it unanimously voted to expel him.[10] And on a number of occasions thereafter, members of Congress have expressed concern that some of their colleagues held other offices after election and even while seated.[11]

Congress has held considerably different views on this subject in recent years, for the fear of its members' being "tainted" by the executive branch no longer seems as great as it once was. Members of Congress, for example, now expect to be included in international meetings, along with officials from the executive branch. And holding a commission in one of the armed-service reserve components is no longer a reason for ousting a legislator, even though a major general in the Air Force Reserve (such as Senator Barry Goldwater) might espouse the cause of that branch of the service. Article I, section 6 is by no means inoperative, but it is no longer as stringently applied as it was in the Van Ness case.

Both the guaranty clause of Article IV, section 4 and the decision of the Supreme Court in *Luther* v. *Borden* (1849) point to another disqualification. This clause which guarantees "to every State in the Union a republican form of government," underlay the Court's statement that "when the senators and representatives of a state are admitted into the councils of the

---

[10] *Debates and Proceedings of the U.S. Congress*, 7th Congress, 2d sess., p. 389 (1802), reel no. 3 (Ann Arbor: University Microfilms, 1955).

[11] See, for example, the test case against Samuel Herrick in 1817. In all, ten Representatives had been elected while they were holding offices within the executive branch and relinquished them just prior to taking the oath of office. Herrick's case was decided in his favor, 77 to 74, but the other nine representatives were permitted to vote on the case (ibid., pp. 1440–1441 [1817], reel no. 7). Also see the Baker and Yell cases, during the Mexican War, in which both men accepted commissions in their states' volunteer forces without resigning from Congress. Although the House was intent upon declaring them ineligible, its hands were tied by patriotic and humanitarian considerations. Yell was killed in action, and by declaring him ineligible the House would have deprived his orphaned children of the travel and per diem allowance due their father as a member of Congress (16 *Congressional Globe* 94, 339, 527, 881 [1847]).

Union, the authority of the government under which they are appointed, as well as its republican character, is recognized by the proper constitutional authority."[12] Since Congress, in seating senators and representatives, thereby acknowledges that their states have republican governments, it may also disqualify senators and representatives elected from states that do not have a republican form of government. In the latter event, it would not matter that these men met the age, citizenship, and inhabitancy requirements. Evidence of this corollary is the refusal of the Senate to seat Joshua Hill and H. V. M. Miller in 1869: Georgia was refused representation in Congress until, as stated by Senate Bill 3, "that State had a republican government elected under its new constitution."[13]

The last two provisions relating to qualifications are Article VI, clause 3 of the Constitution and section 3 of the Fourteenth Amendment. The former requires that all public officials, national and state, "shall be bound by oath or affirmation to support this Constitution." In *Bond et al.* v. *Floyd et al.* (1966), Chief Justice Warren interpreted this clause to mean that a "legislator of course can be required to swear to support the Constitution of the United States as a condition to holding office."[14] While this case dealt with the Georgia House of Representatives' refusal to seat Julian Bond, Chief Justice Warren's statement may be generalized to include national and state legislators alike, since all are required by this constitutional provision to take the same oath.

Closely related to the oath provision of Article VI, clause 3 is the subject matter of the Fourteenth Amendment, section 3:

No person shall be a Senator or Representative . . . who, having previously taken an oath . . . to support the Constitution of the United States, shall have engaged in insurrection or rebellion against the same, or given aid or comfort to the enemies thereof.

This provision also authorizes Congress, after a two-thirds vote, to remove the disqualification from those to whom it may apply. In 1898, during the Spanish-American War, Congress removed this disqualification from onetime members of the Confederacy in an effort to create national harmony and unity.

---

[12] Luther v. Borden, 7 How. 1, 42 (1849).
[13] 40 *Congressional Globe* 2 (1868) and 41 ibid. 103 (1869).
[14] 87 S. Ct. 339, 347.

Because the Fourteenth Amendment was a direct consequence of America's experiences with slavery, secession, and the Civil War, disqualification under section 3 might now be regarded as a dead letter. In fact, however, it is still an operative part of the Constitution—not something applicable only to Jefferson Davis and Robert E. Lee and their compatriots. Indeed, it was this section that the House used against Victor Berger in 1919 and 1920. First elected to Congress in 1910, he had taken the oath required by Article VI, clause 3, and his later antiwar activities and "seditious" conduct in violation of the statute of 1917 were interpreted as giving "aid or comfort to the enemies" of the United States.[15]

So explicit are these five provisions that we must reject the claim of Professor Warren and the Supreme Court that a house may judge members-elect only on grounds of age, citizenship, and inhabitancy.[16] Any one of the eight provisions may be grounds for excluding a congressman-elect. Nor does it matter whether some are designated qualifications and others disqualifications. The consequence for a member-elect is the same no matter which test he fails to meet.

Questions Suggested by the Prohibition of Religious Tests

Article VI, clause 3 of the Constitution forbids a religious test "as a qualification to any office or public trust under the United States." However, in the *absence* of such a constitutional prohibition, who would have had the authority to impose a religious test as a condition for being a member of Congress, or the President, or a federal judge? For merely by prohibiting a religious test for holding national office this provision implies the power to add to the list of constitutional qualifications. If, as Professor Warren claims, the Constitution is all inclusive in its qualifications for congressmen, why was it necessary to make this prohibition?

---

[15] See the debates on Nov. 10, 1919, in 58 *Congressional Record* 8701 (1919).

[16] In Powell v. McCormack, the Court acknowledges my contention. See 89 S. Ct. 1944, 1963, n. 41 (1969), where it cites my article, "A Commentary on the Constitutional Issues in the Powell and Related Cases," 17 *Journal of Public Law* 103, 111–115 (1968). It then states: "We need not reach this question, however, since both sides agree that Powell was not ineligible under any of these provisions."

There is no evidence in *Madison's Journal* of what the delegates had in mind by stipulating this prohibition, nor is there any indication to whom (Congress, the states, or the people) this prohibition was intended to apply. It might, of course, have been only the statement of a principle already current in American thinking. Nevertheless, it suggests various questions about religious qualification.

The principle contained in this clause was introduced to the convention on August 20, 1787 (less than a month before the conclusion of proceedings), when Charles Pinckney submitted several resolutions for the consideration of his colleagues, including one that stated: "No religious test or qualification shall ever be annexed to any oath of office under the authority of the U.S."[17] However, no action was taken on it until August 30, when Pinckney again proposed, as an amendment to the oath clause: "But no religious test shall ever be required as a qualification to any office or public trust under the authority of the United States." Only Pinckney and Morris explicitly endorsed the proposal, but the only critical statement, by Roger Sherman, was directed not to its substance but to its noncontingency, "the prevailing liberty being a sufficient security against such tests."[18]

The information in the record leaves two questions unanswered: (1) against whom was this prohibition to operate? and (2) why had such a prohibitory statement been necessary? With respect to the first question, it would appear that Congress is the only source of additional qualifications. The second question suggests, however, that the Constitution is not all inclusive in providing qualifications.

Only Congress could have instigated a religious qualification in the absence of this prohibitory clause. While voters may as individuals or as groups of like-minded persons judge a candidate by his religious affiliation, they cannot prescribe qualifications for holding national office. States, however, have imposed additional qualifications, requiring that a representative reside within the district from which he is elected[19] and prohibiting state

---

[17] *Madison's Journal*, p. 572.

[18] Ibid., p. 647.

[19] This was the issue in the McCreery case in 1807. John Randolph proposed that the Maryland residency statute be approved by the House, but his proposal was overwhelmingly defeated, 92 to 8 (*Debates and Proceedings of the U.S. Congress*, 10th Congress, 1st sess., p. 890 [1807], reel no. 4).

officials from seeking other offices during the terms for which they were elected or for a stipulated period thereafter.[20] But the House and the Senate have refused to be bound by qualifications set by the states. Besides, the prohibition against religious tests is applicable to all national offices, and the states are scarcely in a position to set qualifications for the President or Chief Justice.

If the no-religious-test clause was intended to protect future Americans from a religious-test constitutional amendment, the Founding Fathers would have incorporated another proviso in Article V of the Constitution, limiting the exercise of constituent power still further. The article provided

that no amendment which may be made prior to the year One thousand Eight hundred and eight shall in any manner affect the first and fourth clauses in the ninth section of the first Article; and that no State, without its consent, shall be deprived of its equal suffrage in the Senate.

Only by a similar proviso might the delegates have prohibited religious qualifications from being introduced by constitutional amendment. And thus Congress is the only agency that might have imposed a religious qualification for all national officers. (This matter will be elaborated below when we consider the significance of the enactment of the First Congress in 1790 and note developments in 1853 and 1862 as further illustrations of what Congress may do under its legislative powers.)

In concluding this discussion about the prohibition of a religious test we should note that its incorporation in the Constitution received more than passing attention from the delegates. For one thing, the Committee on Style (comprised of Morris, Madison, Hamilton, Johnson, and King) made a minor change in Pinckney's wording of this clause, which had been approved by the convention on August 30, 1787. Instead of "under the authority of the United States," the Committee on Style substituted "under the United States."

No matter what is offered for the how and why of this clause, it is an operative part of the Constitution. And by prohibiting a

---

[20] Lyman Trumbull of Illinois resigned a state judgeship about eighteen months before he was elected to the Senate, but if narrowly construed, a provision in the state constitution rendered him ineligible. While the issue is not clear cut in his case, it is evident that most senators opposed the states' adding to the qualifications of congressmen. See the debate in 25 *Congressional Globe* 58, 343, 466, 514–564 (1855).

specific qualification, it implies that Congress has the authority to add others that are not prohibited. This argument is another point that undermines Professor Warren's thesis.

Pertinency of the Criminal Act of 1790

In 1790 the First Congress enacted a comprehensive criminal law dealing with treason, felonies committed on United States property, crimes on the high seas, counterfeiting, and with accessories to the foregoing crimes. Section 21 of this statute defines as a criminal offense the offering of a bribe "to obtain or procure the opinion, judgment, or decree of any judge or judges of the United States, in any suit, controversy, matter, or cause." Persons convicted under this section, including federal judges found guilty of accepting bribes, are subject to its criminal penalties and "forever . . . disqualified to hold any office of honor, trust, or profit under the United States."[21] Only in this provision of the act is there such a disqualification, inasmuch as death was the prescribed punishment for treason and counterfeiting. Even though the provision is unique, it undermines the claim that Congress is without power to prescribe additional qualifications (or disqualifications) by statute.

Of the several factors that should be discussed with respect to this statute of 1790, it is more than a little significant that it appears to be an early application of the doctrine of implied powers. While there is no public policy section that suggests the constitutional bases for the various provisions of the 1790 criminal statute, the sources for most of them are readily apparent. For example, the Constitution specifically authorizes Congress to define offenses—counterfeiting, piracies, felonies on the high seas, and misconduct at United States "forts, magazines, arsenals, dockyards, and other needful buildings"—and to prescribe the punishments for treason as well as for these other offenses. But nowhere in the Constitution is Congress empowered to define bribery of judges as a criminal offense and to prescribe punishments for those who offer and those who accept bribes. Conse-

---

[21] "An Act for the Punishment of Certain Crimes against the United States," *Debates and Proceedings of the U.S. Congress*, 1st Congress, 2d sess., appendix, pp. 2219–2220 (1790), reel no. 1. See also chap. 9, 2 Stat. 112 (1790).

quently, this section of the 1790 statute must have been derived by implication from Congress's powers to create inferior courts, to establish the size of the Supreme Court, and to define the latter's appellate jurisdiction (as well as the jurisdictions of the other federal courts). Similarly, in enacting or providing the punishment of permanent disqualification for national office, Congress used the doctrine of implied powers and thereby established a precedent to which subsequent Congresses might refer.

A second matter relates to the membership of the First Congress if it is contended that this statute proves no more than that Congress usurped a power not intended for it by the Founding Fathers. Members of the House during that session of Congress who were also Founding Fathers were James Madison, Elbridge Gerry, Roger Sherman, George Clymer, Daniel Carroll, and Abraham Baldwin. And almost half of the Senate was comprised of men who had served as delegates to the Constitutional Convention: John Langdon, William S. Johnson, Oliver Ellsworth, Robert Morris, William Few, William Paterson, Richard Bassett, George Read, Pierce Butler, and Rufus King. Therefore this action of the First Congress, in which so many of the Founding Fathers participated, casts serious doubt on the claim that additional qualifications or disqualifications may not be prescribed in statutes.

If Congress could prescribe a permanent disqualification in the Act of 1790, using the doctrine of implied powers in conjunction with its specified powers to create federal courts inferior to the Supreme Court and to define jurisdictions, why may it not prescribe still other qualifications or disqualifications under other specified powers?

In 1853, enacting a bill "to prevent Frauds upon the Treasury of the United States," Congress again provided disqualification as penalties for misconduct by public officials. Section 5 of the act declared it a crime for any public official who has custody of certain records, documents, and papers to destroy them. One of the penalties is that he be "forever afterwards disqualified from holding any office under the Government of the United States."[22] The same penalty was prescribed in section 6 for anyone convicted of offering a bribe to influence national decisions and for

---

[22] *Congressional Globe* appendix 338 (1853).

any public official convicted of accepting a bribe.[23] The test-oath law of July 1862 added a similar disqualification.[24]

There is no evidence that the Act of 1790 was cited as a precedent and justification for Congress's enlarging the list of qualifications and disqualifications in any of the cases that arose in the late eighteenth century and much of the nineteenth century. Indeed, the first recorded reference to the Act of 1790 was on March 4, 1856, when the Senate concerned itself with the eligibility of Lyman Trumbull of Illinois. During the debates on that occasion, Senator Stuart of Michigan cited the act in support of his argument that qualifications are not fixed, and therefore Congress (and state legislatures) may add to them.[25]

Even today the House and Senate, with few exceptions, claim the authority to add to the prescribed constitutional qualifications. The attitude of most members is expressed in a statement by Representative Gerald Ford, who said during the Powell hearings:

> Unfortunately, during the course of this debate, statements have been made which would indicate, if not challenged, that this Congress has the power to exclude a Member-elect only if such Member-elect does not satisfy the three constitutional qualifications [of age, citizenship, and inhabitancy]. I do not believe that the historical record of the precedents of this House support this conclusion.[26]

Minority Leader Ford is not without support in this assertion, for similar claims to broad discretionary authority have been made by other prominent congressmen in previous cases.[27] However, while he and others lay claim to a supporting historical record, they must at least acknowledge that it is spotty and erratic. In the twentieth-century cases, members of Congress have claimed the power to judge their members on grounds other than those specified in the Constitution. But this has not *always* been true, for this prerogative of each house evolved through

---

[23] Ibid.

[24] The provisions of this act and the attendant debates are found in 32 ibid. 2560–3088 (1862).

[25] *Congressional Globe* 563 (1856).

[26] *Congressional Record* H. 1920 (1967).

[27] See, for example, the debates in the Berger case, 58 ibid. 8701 (1919) and the statements by Senators Alben Barkley, 87 ibid. 3 (1941), George, 88 ibid. 2475 (1942), and Ferguson, 93 ibid. 74 (1947).

many cases and over a long period of time. We must, therefore, examine the instances in earlier years when either the House or the Senate was faced with the question of adding to the constitutional qualifications.

Earlier in this chapter we noted the claims of Professor Charles Warren, whose views as an acknowledged authority on the Constitution carry great weight—as in the brief presented in Powell's behalf to the Celler committee and the Supreme Court's decision in *Powell* v. *McCormack*. Citing Professor Warren as its authority, the Powell brief declared:

> The history of the proceedings of the Convention during which the age, citizenship and inhabitancy qualifications were accepted reveals the clear intention of the Enactors that the legislature was to have no power to alter or add to the constitutional qualifications.[28]

A similar claim was made by the Supreme Court in 1969.

Prestigious though they are, there are reasons for questioning such statements. First, instead of just three there are eight qualifications (or disqualifications) in the Constitution. Second, Professor Warren states that, both singly and collectively, the chambers of Congress were denied the power to prescribe additional qualifications; but the Act of 1790 contradicts at least part of his claim: the First Congress, using the doctrine of implied powers, added a specific disqualification by statute. We are hardly in a position, in the twentieth century, to deny Congress the power to prescribe additional qualifications by statute in view of this precedent. Professor Warren makes the denial to a single house contingent upon what he found was a prohibition against Congress as a whole,[29] but inasmuch as his conclusion regarding a denial to the whole Congress is in doubt, the inference from that conclusion is also open to question. This doubt is substantiated by the third point made in this chapter: If Congress is prohibited from adding to the list of constitutional qualifications, why was it necessary to prohibit a religious test as a condition for holding national office?

---

[28] *In re Adam Clayton Powell: Hearings before Select Committee pursuant to H. Res. 1*, p. 7.

[29] "For certainly [the Convention] did not intend that a single branch of Congress should possess a power which the Convention had expressly refused to vest in the whole Congress: (Warren, op. cit) p. 421.

For the reasons we have stated, we can claim that Congress *does* have the power to prescribe additional qualifications by statute. But a question remains: May either chamber more or less arbitrarily devise a new qualification for a new situation? To determine how the House and Senate have answered this question, we must trace historical developments from 1789 to 1967, which we will do in the next four chapters.

III

Defining the Dimensions of Congressional Power, 1789 to 1860

Precedents, a major feature of American constitutional history, also played important roles in determining the boundaries of Congress's quasi-judicial powers. Indeed, given the inexact language of the Constitution and the specific questions that demanded answers, it became apparent virtually at the outset that each house would have to define the scope and nature of its powers as situations arose. This led, of course, to the development of self-defined boundaries, and thus to the possibility that constitutional powers would be exercised in arbitrary fashion. The question, then, is whether each chamber realized not only the likely consequences of its actions in such situations—as well as for the future—but how seriously its exercise of power might affect the value of representative government.

In considering such matters, we will direct our attention to (1) how and with what consistency each chamber applied the constitutional qualifications for membership; (2) how the factors of time and place figured in the early uses of their quasi-judicial powers; (3) the extent to which either house sought to broaden its powers, especially by establishing tests of fitness other than the qualifications specified in the Constitution; and (4) how a precedent, once created, might take on larger dimensions and thereby contribute to a further expansion of congressional powers.

Neither the House nor the Senate had to operate entirely in a vacuum at the beginning. Since seven of the eight qualifications and disqualifications were part of the Constitution at the time it took effect in 1789, each house could have acted on more than a member-elect's age, citizenship, and state of residence. Each house, furthermore, could have referred to the clause prohibiting religious tests, seeing in it an implied authorization to prescribe additional qualifications. And after 1790, there was the precedent created by the First Congress, which prescribed an additional disqualification by statute. Thus each house was in a position to use a broad definition of its powers in judging the qualifications of its members.

Defining the dimensions of the other aspects of their quasi-judicial powers was necessarily more difficult; not even the scanty constitutional guidelines of age, etc., were available to either house in deciding at or by what *time* a member must meet the constitutional requirements. Nor were there guidelines to assist a chamber in deciding whether it could punish a member for an act of misconduct committeed prior to his election or away from the halls of Congress. What one house offered as an answer to either the time or place questions would therefore be expected to serve as a guideline on later occasions.

Except for prescribing an additional disqualification in the criminal act of 1790, how did each chamber define its quasi-judicial powers in the earliest cases? An answer to this question can be found only by examining all the landmark cases decided between 1789 and 1860. Within that seventy-one-year period, each chamber had a number of opportunities to define not only its power to judge the qualifications of members-elect but its other powers as well. The number and the nature of such cases are shown in the accompanying charts, which identify only the instances in which the House and the Senate exercised their powers to judge both the constitutional and extra-constitutional qualifications and the conduct of their members, including actions that took place before their election to Congress. The many instances in which questions were raised about the elections and returns of members are not included.

Between 1789 (when the first contested election cases were heard) and 1967 (when the seating of a Republican from Georgia was challenged),[1] several hundred such incidents commanded the attention of Congress. And because contested elections involve either unintentional human error or outright fraud, they were no doubt carefully investigated by the House and the Senate. Also, because of their procedural questions, their implications for representative government, and the possibility that contested elections may be resolved on partisan grounds, they are appropriate subjects for continuing study by scholars. But only a few contested elections will command our attention in this study, and only when they pertain to the questions this study has posed.

This study, the reader should remember, is undertaken as a historical analysis of only one facet of American constitutional development; it is not a study of legislative behavior. Consequently, when we encounter inconsistencies in a chamber's application of the qualification tests, we will accept them as they are rather than make judgments about how legislators respond to political or other stimuli. What is most important to us is how each house came to regard its power and how inconsistencies created a bifurcated rather than an integrated base of precedents. Therefore, as more and more cases became part of the historical record, the House and the Senate could move in any direction they wanted in specific cases and still claim the sanction of precedents.

Constitutional Qualifications

There were few instances in which a member-elect was challenged as disqualified by reason of the age, citizenship, or inhabitancy requirements of the Constitution. On the other hand, there were many instances in which a chamber had to resolve questions

---

[1] Benjamin Blackburn's right to membership was questioned in 1967. Although he was sworn, it was with the understanding that a committee would investigate and determine whether he had been properly elected (113 *Congressional Record* 4, 16 [1967]). The validity of his election was later established.

about a member who held a second office. All such cases provided opportunities for interpreting constitutional provisions and were presumed to serve as precedents. They also reveal how partisan and other considerations played important roles, in some instances justifying the use of a power that was not consistently employed.

An important factor in cases that involved constitutional qualifications was the time factor. By what time must an individual have met the age, citizenship, and inhabitancy requirements? By what time must an individual have relinquished a post within the executive branch in order not to violate the prohibition against holding two offices?

Age *could* have been a factor when Henry Clay presented his credentials to the Senate on December 29, 1806. Clay, born on April 12, 1777, was three and one-half months short of thirty years when he was given the oath of office. Indeed, he was not eligible to be a senator even when that session of Congress ended, on March 3, 1807. (Apparently this fact was known to others, for Stephen Douglas made reference to the Clay matter many years later in arguing for the seating of his colleague from Illinois, James Shields.) However, Clay's eligibility was not challenged;[2] but the Senate did not show the same leniency to Albert Gallatin in 1794 and James Shields in 1849, who at the time they presented their credentials as senators-elect were several months short of meeting the citizenship requirement.

Gallatin, who immigrated in 1780 and served the Revolutionary cause, had not rendered a formal oath of allegiance until October 1785. When he presented his credentials in December 1793, he was ten months short of fulfilling the citizenship requirement. Thus Gallatin, a naturalized citizen of the United States at the time the Constitution was adopted, was eligible to be President (under Article II, section 1 of the Constitution) but was ineligible for membership in the Senate. However, partisan rather than patriotic factors dictated the Senate's response to the

---

[2] The governor of Kentucky appointed Clay to serve the unexpired term (one session) of Senator John Adair; his credentials were accepted Dec. 29, 1806, and he participated in Senate business until Mar. 3, 1807. See *Debates and Proceedings of the U.S. Congress*, 9th Congress, 2d sess., p. 24 and passim (1806), reel no. 4 (Ann Arbor: University Microfilms, 1955).

eligibility question. Although Gallatin was given the oath of office on December 2, 1793, he was unseated on February 28, 1794. By a vote of 14 to 12, the Federalist-dominated Senate ousted this political enemy, a Jeffersonian Republican.[3]

At least three questions are suggested by the Gallatin case, two of which were answered not by what the Senate said or claimed but by the way it acted. First, since Gallatin had been formally sworn and had functioned as a senator for approximately three months, was it not necessary that he be expelled by a two-thirds vote instead of being unseated by a mere majority? Second, since for all intents and purposes he was an acting though ineligible senator, were the decisions in which he participated valid? Third, when a member-elect is challenged by reason of his eligibility, are his credentials to be accepted, the oath of office administered, and only later is an inquiry to be launched into his qualifications?

The first two questions were answered by the Senate's action, which implied that a person who is ineligible for membership at the time he is sworn remains so thereafter; consequently he can be removed by majority vote. Also implicit was a distinction between a *de jure* member, who can only be expelled, and a *de facto* member, who is ineligible from the moment he is seated but whose status does not affect the decisions in which he participated. The third question was not directly applicable to Gallatin, the issue of his eligibility having been raised only after his credentials were accepted.

The implications of Gallatin's case later became explicit in statements by Stephen Douglas in 1849 and by Scott Lucas in 1942. Without substantiating his claim, Douglas reported that statutes had been enacted by narrow margins while a *de facto* member was sitting but this had not affected their validity.[4] In 1942, Senator Lucas cited the Gallatin case as a precedent for his

---

[3] Ibid., 3d Congress, 1st sess., p. 57 (1794), reel no. 2. Actually, Gallatin's was not the first "citizenship" case; in 1789 the House had to decide whether William Smith of South Carolina fulfilled the citizenship requirement. Prior to the Revolution, Smith went to Europe to study, and he did not return until after the peace treaty of 1783. The House decided that he was eligible for membership.

[4] See 18 *Congressional Globe* 338–350 (1849), in which the question about *de jure* and *de facto* status was explored.

committee's recommendation that William Langer be unseated. The Gallatin case, he said, was an example of the Senate's excluding

a man who had already been seated. Acting under its authority to judge the qualifications of its members, it excluded him by majority vote because of a disqualification specified in the Constitution.[5]

Although the third question (about accepting credentials) was variously answered by Congress on other occasions, the usual practice was to accept the credentials as *prima facie* evidence that a member-elect had a valid claim to a seat.[6] It was this practice that Stephen Douglas relied upon in arguing that General James Shields be seated in March 1849. Neither prior service in state office nor duty with the Illinois volunteers in the Mexican War was considered sufficient justification for the Senate to waive the citizenship requirement in Shields's case.

Naturalized in October 1840, Shields had not yet met the citizenship requirement when he presented his credentials to the Senate on March 4, 1849. But there were two ways by which Shields might prevent the invalidation of his election. First, he could claim that he had acquired citizenship before 1840 because his father had been naturalized prior to that year and James Shields, as a minor, would have become a citizen at the same time. Since the Senate expressed little sympathy for this claim, Shields had to pursue an alternative course of action. He hoped to delay the Senate's decision until the following December, at which time the question would presumably become moot. Whether this alternative really held promise for Shields depended on how the Senate answered the question: At what

[5] 88 *Congressional Record* 2402 (1942).

[6] Both the Bilbo (1947) and the Powell (1967) cases show that this has not always been the practice; the credentials of neither man were accepted, nor was the oath of office given (93 *Congressional Record* 108 [1947] and 113 ibid. 143 [1967]). But in 1941, Langer's credentials *were* accepted. Majority Leader Barkley stated that "the better practice in such cases seems to have been to allow the Senator-elect to take the oath without prejudice, which means without prejudice to him and without prejudice to the Senate." If charges are later proved against the senator, Barkley said, the members may by majority vote decide "his fitness and qualifications" (87 ibid. 3 [1941]). Approximately fifteen months were given to the Langer case before his claim was upheld. This long delay was at least one reason for deciding to exclude Bilbo from the very beginning of the Bilbo debates.

time must a member-elect fulfill the constitutional requirements? At least in March, the time factor was critical. On January 13, 1849, Shields had been elected by the Illinois General Assembly to a six-year term "commencing on the fourth day of March 1849." Although a new Congress commenced on that date in odd-number years, the first session usually convened in December; and the Senate was meeting in special session—an extension of the Thirtieth Congress—when Shields presented his credentials on March 4. Had he awaited the first session of the Thirty-first Congress in the following December, the question about his eligibility may not have been raised, but by presenting his credentials in March, Shields prompted a challenge to his eligibility and a debate over the time factor.

Debate over the latter question was necessary since the precedents were, at best, inadequate in providing answers; and three distinctive positions emerged. Stephen Douglas argued that the Senate should construe the citizenship requirement liberally—taking no challenge whatever, just as it had done when it seated Clay and Andrew Jackson.[7] This was the essence of Senator Butler's position as well, who believed that the Senate should postpone action until December, at which time the issue would be moot. Different arguments were presented by Daniel Webster, who claimed that a member-elect had to be eligible at the time of his election. And John C. Calhoun contended that qualifications had to be fulfilled by the beginning of a new Congress (March 4), with which the Senate concurred. In a resolution, Shields's election was declared void because of his

not having been a citizen of the United States the term of years required as a qualification to be a Senator of the United States at the commencement of the term for which he was elected.[8]

---

[7] Douglas claimed that Jackson was underage when he was elected to the Senate (in 1797) and that he awaited his thirtieth birthday before presenting his credentials, but according to one of his biographers, James Parton, Jackson was born on Mar. 15, 1767 (*The Life of Andrew Jackson* [1887]). Thus Jackson would have been thirty on Mar. 15, 1797. However, Jackson was elected by the Tennessee General Assembly to fill the vacancy created by the resignation of William Cocke, who was not admitted to membership until May 15, 1797. When Jackson presented his credentials as Cocke's successor, on Nov. 22, he was several months beyond his thirtieth birthday.

[8] 18 *Congressional Globe* appendix 338–351 (1849).

Despite this definitive answer in March 1849, Shields's credentials were accepted the following December 3, even though they proclaimed that he had been "elected a Senator by the Legislature of Illinois for the term of six years, commencing on the fourth day of March 1849."[9]

Seldom were the issues as clear cut as they were in the Gallatin and the Shields cases. Although the eligibility of Philip Barton Key (1808) and John Bailey (1824) was questioned by reason of inhabitancy, other issues were also raised. Inasmuch as the latter were primary and important issues, they probably determined the thinking of many representatives in voting against the seating of Key and Bailey.

Key had joined the British forces after the signing of the Declaration of Independence and had received half-pay as a British captain from 1783 through 1805, actions which involved questions about constitutional and extra-constitutional qualifications. After investigating all the issues in the Key case, the Committee on Elections recommended that he be declared eligible for membership, but the narrow margin by which this recommendation was approved by the House, 57 to 52, suggests how concerned many members were about the charges.

Leaving the extra-constitutional issues aside for the moment, we will consider the question of inhabitancy. Was Key an inhabitant of Maryland at the time of his election? For some time prior to his election, in 1806, Key had resided in the District of Columbia, but he owned property in Montgomery County, Maryland, where he began building a second home in 1806. Just prior to the election, he moved into this partially completed house. After the election, he returned to the District of Columbia.[10]

The facts in this case, Representative John Randolph and others argued, warranted Key's exclusion. Were Key to be admitted to membership, they warned, other men, sent by influential and wealthy groups "for a few days' residence into any State in the Union," would also become eligible for election. By voting for Key, the majority of the representatives indicated that inhabitancy is a condition that can be met only at the moment of election.

---

[9] 19 ibid., p. 1.
[10] *Debates and Proceedings of the U.S. Congress*, 10th Congress, 1st sess., pp. 803, 1058, 1149, 1489–1496, 1845–1849 (1808), reel no. 4.

In 1824, John Bailey could not meet even this minimal residency condition. For six years prior to his election he had been employed as a clerk in the Department of State and had resided in the District of Columbia, but his home, he argued, was in Massachusetts. He neither owned property nor participated in civic affairs in Washington. On the other hand, his personal property was kept in "his room" at his father's home in Massachusetts. Therefore, Bailey told the House, he should be regarded as a bona fide resident of the Massachusetts district from which he was elected. Precedents, Bailey believed, supported his claim to membership; other men who had served in various United States posts had been elected to and seated in Congress. Indeed, another representative-elect, John Forsyth of Georgia, had been elected to that same Congress while serving as minister plenipotentiary in Madrid.

If Bailey's and Forsyth's were analogous situations, the two identical questions can be posed of each. Is a government employee who serves either in the nation's capital or elsewhere an inhabitant of the state from which he is elected? And if a man is elected to Congress while he holds office within the executive branch, is he rendered ineligible by reason of the constitutional prohibition against holding two offices?

But the Bailey and the Forsyth cases were not regarded as analogous, as is shown by their disposition. By a vote of 125 to 55, Bailey was declared ineligible on the ground that he did not meet the inhabitancy requirement.[11] At the same time, the House tabled a resolution on Forsyth's eligibility. Obviously, then, the first question was answered one way for Bailey and another way for Forsyth. Thus the House made a distinction between the offices these men previously held, just as it differentiated between the reasons why neither man resided within his state at the time of his election.

Possibly the House should also have addressed itself to the second question. On occasion, congressmen had admitted that the second-office prohibition was necessary to prevent the chief executive from gaining an unwarranted voice in legislative matters, and it was for that reason that Van Ness was unseated in

---

[11] Ibid., 18th Congress, 1st sess., pp. 1794–1803 (1824), reel no. 10. Later, Bailey was elected in a special election and seated in the second session.

HOUSE QUALIFICATIONS AND DISQUALIFICATIONS, CONSTITUTIONAL AND
EXTRA-CONSTITUTIONAL, 1789–1860
(Including Charges of Misconduct as a Member)

Type of Issue	No. of Cases	Seated	Not Seated	Move to Expel	Expelled or Unseated	Resigned	Reelected and Seated	Punishment: Censure, Rebuke,
Constitutional								
Age	0							
Citizenship	1	1						
Inhabitancy	2	1	1				1	
Holding another office	4				1			Outcome indecisi
	(Plus 10 cases not acted upon)							
Extra-Constitutional								
State proceedings in elections	2	2				1		
Service to another government	1	(Philip Barton Key [also included above under "Inhabitancy"]						
Misconduct								
Before election	2	2						
While a member in chamber	23				2			18
Away from chamber	12				3	7	3	1

1802. His second office, the noncompensated post of major in
the militia of the District of Columbia, was not such as to bias his
voting in Congress. Nevertheless, to permit Van Ness to remain a
member, said one of his colleagues, would be to "establish a
precedent which may hereafter be attended with pernicious consequences." By unanimously voting to unseat Van Ness the
House had proved, Randolph said, that it wanted to remove
"even the shadow of Executive influence."[12]

When should a chamber be concerned about "the shadow of
Executive influence"? When a sitting member accepts a second
office? When a person is elected to Congress while holding an
office in the executive branch? Or when a member-elect continues
in his executive-branch office until just prior to taking the oath as
a congressman? In 1824, during the debates over Bailey's eligi-

---

[12] Ibid., 7th Congress, 2d sess., p. 399 (1802), reel no. 3.

SENATE QUALIFICATIONS AND DISQUALIFICATIONS, CONSTITUTIONAL AND
EXTRA-CONSTITUTIONAL, 1789–1860
(Including Charges of Misconduct as a Member)

Type of Issue	No. of Cases	Seated	Not Seated	Move to Expel	Expelled or Unseated	Resigned	Reelected and Seated	Punishment: Censure, Rebuke, Apology
Constitutional								
Age	2							
Citizenship	2	1	1		1			
Inhabitancy	(Not made an issue)							
Holding another office								
Extra-Constitutional								
State proceedings in elections	4	4			1		1	
Service to another government	1				1			
Other	1	1						
Misconduct								
Before election	4	4						
While a member in chamber	2							
Away from chamber	3			1		1		

bility, Representative Storrs proposed that the second-office prohibition be discussed. He was obviously anxious about presidential influence, but there was a second reason for his proposal.
This was the first time since 1817 that the House had been
confronted with a second-office issue, and Storrs wanted his
colleagues to correct a decision of that year retroactively.

In 1817 it had been proposed in the House that the Committee
on Elections determine how many members-elect held or accepted offices within the executive branch between the previous
March 4 and the opening of the first session in December.
Accordingly, a communication from President Monroe identified
ten representatives who had held posts within the executive
branch after March 4, 1817. All but one of them formally resigned this post prior to taking the oath as a congressman. In all
ten instances there were identical questions to be answered. May
a person seek election to Congress while continuing in an office
under the United States? And may a man retain this office

between March 4, the date a new Congress begins, and December, when Congress actually convenes?

Two test cases were heard by the House. Samuel Herrick of Ohio, who had been an attorney of the United States at the time of his election, did not resign that office until November 29, 1817, just prior to the convening of Congress. George Mumford, who served as principal assessor for the United States in his home district in North Carolina, never formally resigned that office, not even at the time he presented his credentials to Congress. The Committee on Elections, which reported favorably for each man, declared that Herrick had not rendered himself ineligible by retaining his post as attorney until November 29. In Mumford's case, the committee reported, a formal resignation was unnecessary, the duties and compensation of his previous office having ended at the moment he took the oath as a representative.

Although a House majority sustained Herrick's claim to membership, both the narrow vote (77 to 74) and an unusual procedure raised doubts with respect to the decision. Mumford and the other eight representatives, whose rights to membership hinged on the disposition of Herrick's claim, were permitted to vote on the issue, and each of these men voted for Herrick.[13]

Because of this unseemly procedure, uncertainty about the time question, and concern over presidential influence, Representative Storrs proposed that the second-office question be considered along with the inhabitancy issue in the Bailey case (1824). However, his failure to convince his colleagues of the need for this larger inquiry led to a further delay in answering questions about the meaning of the second-office prohibition. Not until the Mexican War was there another opportunity to raise such questions. Although in 1847 the House was intent on acting in a definitive manner, the cases that arose during the Mexican War were so complicated by other factors as to affect the representatives' decision.

During the Mexican War, Representatives Baker and Yell accepted commissions in the volunteer forces of their respective states but did not resign from Congress. After being on duty for a

---

[13] Ibid., 15th Congress, 1st sess., p. 1414 (1817), reel no. 7. The relevant documents and debate are found at pp. 422, 515, 543, 855, and 1435.

time in Mexico, Colonel Baker was prevailed upon by his fellow officers to take a leave and return to Congress to obtain greater logistical support for the volunteers—exactly the kind of "outside" influence that had disturbed some representatives in the Van Ness, Herrick, and Bailey cases. And now it was real rather than hypothetical. Because of criticism and demands from his colleagues that he be declared ineligible, Colonel Baker resigned his House seat and returned to Mexico. Thus, although the issue had been rendered moot, the Committee on Elections proposed that Baker be declared ineligible as of the time he accepted the appointment as "colonel of volunteers from the State of Illinois in service of the United States."[14]

Authorities in Arkansas, meanwhile, believing that Yell's acceptance of a commission had created a vacancy in Congress, held a special election and Thomas W. Newton was chosen to succeed Yell. But because Yell had not resigned from Congress, the House was faced with the question whether a vacancy existed and whether Newton should be seated. The Committee on Elections, recommending that both Baker and Yell be declared ineligible and Newton be sworn, committed itself to a strict construction of the second-office clause, and the fact that the House did not act on the committee's recommendation must be attributed to extraneous circumstances rather than to disagreement among the members. After Yell's death on the battlefield, the House was informed that his children were orphaned, destitute, and ineligible for public assistance under the federal pension programs. Thus the House found itself in a dilemma. If it voted for the committee's resolution it would deny the children the mileage and per diem allowances that were due their father as a member of the Twenty-ninth Congress. Under these circumstances, the House took no action on the recommendation; and by seating Newton it did no more than acknowledge that a vacancy was created by Yell's death.

Such was the outcome of the first cases involving questions about constitutional qualifications. They provided no definitive answers to such questions as these: When must a specified requirement be fulfilled? What constitutes inhabitancy? At what time is a member disqualified by reason of holding a second

---

[14] 16 *Congressional Globe* 527 (1847). See *supra*, Chapter 2, fn. 11.

office? Nor does the evidence show that the constitutional tests were consistently applied. The only conclusion that can be drawn from these several cases is that, for partisan or other reasons, one Congress applied these tests strictly whereas another scarcely noted that it had the power to apply them.

Misconduct of Members in the Halls of Congress

The power of each house to judge the conduct of its members and to punish them is prescribed in Article I, section 5 of the Constitution:

> Each house may determine the rules of its proceedings, punish its members for disorderly behaviour, and, with the concurrence of two thirds, expel a member.

Since this provision begins by authorizing each chamber to prescribe its own rules, do its following clauses imply that a member is subject to punishment, including expulsion, only for interfering with house procedures and for misconduct in chamber? Or does this provision authorize an even greater jurisdiction, permitting the House and the Senate to punish a member for offenses committed elsewhere, or even for misconduct before becoming a member? Thus the factor of place is as significant as the factor of time in defining the jurisdiction of a chamber.

Between 1789 and the outbreak of the Civil War there were many instances in which senators and representatives were charged with misconduct within the halls of Congress, although not solely within their chambers. A number of these cases were quite serious—members fought with canes, brandished pistols, and challenged others to duels. Although on some occasions penalties were demanded by colleagues, the usual practice—as it evolved in the House and became the custom in the Senate as well—was to settle the issues with an apology and let the journals' accounts of the events serve as a public rebuke.

Dueling was such an accepted practice for several decades after the Revolution that members of Congress may have been excused for not regarding this as misconduct. There were occasions, however, in which a challenge to a duel was regarded either as a breach of the privileges of a chamber or as an attempt to compel a member to answer elsewhere "for any speech or debate in either house."[15] The first time a challenge was issued, the House charged that its privileges had been breached.

Senator Gunn of Georgia, who believed that Representative Baldwin (also of Georgia) had a document that was politically damaging to him, demanded that he be given access to it. Baldwin denied having the document. If he had had such a paper, Baldwin wrote to Gunn, he would have made it available to him, if approached in a civil manner. Angered by this response, Gunn issued a challenge through Senator Frelinghuysen of New Jersey, which, transmitted at the bar of the House, led to charges that the privileges of the chamber had been breached. Letters of apology from Senators Gunn and Frelinghuysen closed the issue as far as the House was concerned, and no action was taken by the Senate.[16]

Between 1796, the year Gunn issued his challenge to Baldwin, and 1856, when Representative Brooks caned Senator Sumner into unconsciousness, other acts of misconduct either occurred or originated within a chamber. The first of these acts involved Representatives Lyon and Griswold in 1798. On one occasion Lyon spat upon Griswold, and was bitterly denounced by the genteel Federalists. If the Republicans chose "to associate with such a *kennel of filth*," said Representative Dana of Massachusetts, "let them do so," but he would remove Lyon from Congress "as citizens remove *impurities* and *filth* from their docks and wharves."[17] After a Federalist move to expel Lyon fell short of the required two-thirds (52 to 44), Griswold initiated vengeance on his own. Several days later, just prior to the convening of the House, Griswold attacked Lyon with his cane and the latter responded with firetongs. Other representatives separated the combatants and for the remainder of that day no official notice was taken of the incident.

On the following day, Representative Davis of Kentucky proposed that Griswold and Lyon be expelled. According to Representative Parker, this was the only way to preserve the dignity of

---

[15] Article I, sec. 6 states: ". . . and for any speech or debate in either house, they shall not be questioned in any other places."

[16] Relevant material and reports can be found in *Debates and Proceedings of the U.S. Congress*, 4th Congress, 1st sess., pp. 786–798 (1796), reel no. 2.

[17] Ibid., 5th Congress, 1st sess., p. 1007 (1798), reel no. 2.

the House, for he had encountered Philadelphians on the streets that morning and heard such comments as "There is nothing to do in Congress to-day—there's no fighting going on." But instead of expelling Griswold and Lyon the House adopted a resolution commanding them to abstain from further acts of violence while they were members.[18]

Punishing members for breaching the privileges of the House and thereby protecting its dignity was considered necessary by some members of Congress. However, more than the protection of institutional integrity was at stake. It is a serious incongruity for legislators, who prescribe rules of conduct for society, to commit breaches of peace and order. Also incongruous is the fact that legislators were either censured or were the subjects of censure resolutions even though their offenses were insignificant in comparison to dueling with and killing a fellow legislator, brandishing deadly weapons during heated debates, and cudgeling other members of Congress with cane or fists—all of whom escaped censure.

In 1832, Representative Stanberry commented: "And let me say that I have heard the remark frequently made, that the eyes of the Speaker are too frequently turned from the chair . . . to the white house"—for which he was censured by his colleagues.[19]

John Quincy Adams, in 1842, obedient to the provision in the First Amendment that speaks of the people's right to petition government, barely escaped censure for introducing a petition from forty-five citizens in Massachusetts who, disturbed about slavery, demanded that the Union be dissolved. Because of the "gag rule" against receiving petitions from abolitionists, a resolution to censure Adams was introduced. He was saved from total embarrassment when 106 of his colleagues voted against the resolution—but 93 voted for it.[20]

Not long thereafter, Joshua Giddings of Ohio was censured for introducing a series of resolutions on the *Creole* incident. In 1841, carrying slaves from Virginia to New Orleans, this vessel

---

[18] Ibid., p. 1043.

[19] Gales's and Seaton's *Register of Debates in Congress*, 22d Congress, 1st session, pp. 3876–3887, and 3907–3908 (1832), reel no. 3 (Ann Arbor: University Microfilm Series, 1955).

[20] 11 *Congressional Globe* 168–214 (1842). Later that year Adams unsuccessfully proposed repeal of the "gag law" (12 ibid. 31 [1842]).

had come under the control of mutinous blacks who forced her to be brought within the jurisdiction of the British at Nassau, where the authorities liberated all the slaves who had not been responsible for the murder of a passenger. Although this incident was not finally arbitrated by the United States and Great Britain until 1855, diplomatic negotiations were underway in 1842, at the time Giddings introduced his resolutions claiming that the blacks recovered their freedom when the ship entered international waters. These resolutions, Representative Botts of Virginia contended, touched upon issues sensitive to the negotiations; therefore, he said, Giddings deserved the condemnation of both the American people and of the House. And on March 22, 1842, Giddings was censured.[21] He immediately resigned but was soon reelected by his constituents.

Thus in 1832 and 1842, censure was demanded for Stanberry, Adams, and Giddings. Yet in 1837, when William J. Graves of Kentucky killed Jonathan Cilley of Maine in a duel, the House took no action on a recommendation that Graves be expelled and the other involved representatives be censured.[22] Nor did the Senate take action against Senator Crittenden, who had served as a second.

Between 1837 and 1854 there were a number of violent personal encounters in chamber, involving Bell, Turney, Wise, Stanly, Rathbun, White, Haralson, Jones, Duer, Meade, Brown, Wilcox, Benton, Foote, Polk, White, Churchwell, and Cullom. In two of these encounters (Benton-Foote and Churchwell-Cullom), weapons were drawn. While all of these incidents were cause for alarm for various members, who demanded punishments stronger than an apology, the majority preferred that the incidents be settled on the mildest possible terms.

The report that "deadly weapons" had been drawn in the Churchwell-Cullom encounter caused Preston Brooks to propose, facetiously, that the sergeant at arms erect

---

[21] Ibid., p. 346.

[22] A committee report stated: "It is the highest offence which can be committed against either House of Congress; against the freedom of speech and of debate therein; against the spirit and the substance of that constitutional provision, that for any speech or debate in either House, the members shall not be questioned in any other place, and violates essentially the right of perfect immunity *elsewhere* for words spoken in debate here" (*Congressional Globe* 332 [1837]).

a rack in the rotunda, where members who are addicted to the carrying of concealed weapons, shall be required to place them before entering the Hall, and that they shall be exposed to the inspection of the curious as long as the men are employed in legislation.[23]

But the House might well have adopted a proposal that would have covered all likely weapons, concealed or otherwise—as Brooks himself demonstrated two years later when he caned Senator Sumner. In Brooks's judgment, Sumner had made remarks "libelous of the State of South Carolina, and slanderous of his near kinsman, Mr. Butler, a Senator from that State, who at the time was absent from the Senate and the city."[24] Brooks had hoped to encounter Sumner outside the Capitol Building, but, failing this, he and Representative Keitt invaded the Senate chamber during a recess, Brooks to chastise Sumner and Keitt to keep others from interfering. So violent was the attack, onlookers reported, that Sumner was rendered bloody and senseless.

This attack, a House committee stated, breached the privileges of the Senate. Because the Senate could not punish Brooks, the committee majority stated, action against him became the responsibility of "the House of which he is a member." This majority then recommended that Brooks be expelled and that the House express "disapprobation of the actions" of Representatives Keitt and Edmondson (the latter had been involved only in a minor way).[25] However, the vote to expel Brooks fell short of the required two-thirds (121 to 95) and, after separate votes on Keitt's and Edmondson's conduct, the House censured only the former. Immediately thereafter, Brooks and Keitt resigned, were reelected in special elections, and were seated.

Other Erring Members of Congress

Prior to the Civil War, three other types of misconduct also demanded the attention of the House or Senate from time to time: (1) offenses committed beyond the immediate vicinity of Congress, (2) alleged misconduct before reelections, and (3)

---

[23] 23 ibid. 1466 (1854).

[24] From report of the Select Committee, 25 *Congressional Globe* 1317 (1856).

[25] Pertinent data are in ibid., pp. 1279–1683.

offenses allegedly committed before a member was elected to a first term in Congress.

Senator William Blount became the object of an expulsion resolution in 1797 when President Adams submitted documents to the Senate that implicated him in a plan to incite the Indians against the Spanish and to seize Florida and Louisiana for the British. Since Spain and Great Britain were then at war, this conspiracy affected the neutrality of the United States, and it was also in conflict with a treaty between the United States and Spain. (Both signatories promised to maintain peace and harmony among the Indian nations and to confine them to their respective areas.) Blount's complicity in this plot to incite the Indians prompted his expulsion from the Senate.[26]

Approximately ten years later the Senate heard charges against Senator John Smith, who was cited as a co-conspirator with Aaron Burr. Having no more than a grand jury indictment and depositions from private citizens, some senators hesitated to expel Smith on the mere suspicion of guilt. Nevertheless a substantial vote to expel was compiled and Smith resigned as a consequence of this hostile expression from his colleagues.[27]

Matthew Lyon's problems did not end with the two incidents that almost brought his expulsion from the House in early 1798. Because of the erratic pattern of elections in that day, Lyon was a candidate for reelection in the fall of 1798 even though he still had another year to serve in the Fifth Congress. When the second session of the Fifth Congress was convened in December 1798, Lyon could not attend it because he had been sentenced to a four-month jail term for violation of the Sedition Act of 1798. After his release from jail, Lyon returned to Congress, where he was subjected to a second expulsion move by the Federalists. Lyon's conviction on the sedition charge, said Representative Bayard, was proof that he was "a notorious and seditious person, and of depraved mind, and wicked and diabolical disposition." Republicans, however, viewed Lyon's conviction as persecution for political reasons, and their support made it impossible for the Federalists to get the two-thirds vote required to expel.[28]

---

[26] Relevant materials can be found in *Debates and Proceedings of the U.S. Congress*, 5th Congress, 1st sess., pp. 34–44 (1797), reel no. 2.

[27] Ibid., 10th Congress, 1st sess., p. 42 (1807), reel no. 4.

[28] Ibid., 5th Congress, 2d sess., pp. 2954–2973 (1799), reel no. 2.

Having failed to expel Lyon in the spring of 1799, after his release from prison, the Federalists might have been expected to exclude him when the first session of the Sixth Congress convened in December 1799. The Federalists still had majority control and therefore had enough votes to deny him membership. But neither on that occasion, nor many years later—when Preston Brooks returned to the House on a "vote of confidence" from his constituents—was there any attempt to exclude a member-elect on the ground of his conduct during a previous term in office.

Both Lyon and Brooks had been saved from expulsion by the two-thirds requirement. And although their misconduct and the efforts to expel them had occurred only shortly before they presented new credentials, other members did not seize this opportunity to punish them by exclusion. It is possible, of course, that the House doubted that it had the power to punish its members for misdeeds committed in the past. Such a doubt was formally acknowledged in the 1850s, shortly after the Brooks case, when the House took up a case whose allegations referred to a prior act of misconduct.

After a *New York Times* editorial of January 6, 1857, charged several congressmen with corrupt practices, a select committee investigated the charges, accused three members of Congress of fraudulent practices, and proposed their expulsion. Then, before any action could be taken on the committee's recommendation, Representatives William A. Gilbert, Francis S. Edwards, and Orsamus B. Matteson resigned.[29] But Matteson, having been re-elected to Congress before this incident was brought to light, attended the opening of the Thirty-fifth Congress (December 7, 1857) and was given the oath of office with the other members of the House. Thus the House had a new opportunity to consider whether its power to punish extended to acts of misconduct committed before a man's election or reelection.

On January 15, 1858, it was proposed that an investigation be made of new charges of corruption among legislators. An amendment to this resolution called for action "to complete the purification of the House, and the expurgation of offensive members." Representative Harris of Illinois thereupon proposed that the committee investigate the charges made against Matteson the

---

[29] 26 *Congressional Globe* 760–933 (1857).

previous year and recommend the action "necessary and proper to maintain and vindicate the character of this house."[30] Although this amendment was ruled ungermane to the original resolution, Harris was able to get approval for the investigation of Matteson.

A critical point on this occasion was the implication in the House's approval of the Harris resolution. By adopting it, the majority indicated its belief that the House had the power both to judge a member's past misconduct and to punish him for it. However, and whatever its initial impressions, the majority came to another conclusion after the committee had conducted its investigation and submitted its report. The entire matter was tabled by a vote of 96 to 69.

During the debates on the committee report, two points of view were expressed. The committee's majority, Seward of Georgia reported, was of the opinion that to deny membership to Matteson would be tantamount to limiting and restricting "the sovereign people in the choice of their Representatives." Thus the fact that Matteson's alleged misconduct was brought to light only after his reelection had no apparent relevancy on this occasion. Those who took the contrary position expressed themselves in terms of the right of a legislative body to protect itself against a person who is known to be infamous.[31] While the latter argument, voiced by Craige of North Carolina, had only minority support on this occasion, it was to prevail later.

By not acting against Lyon and Brooks for their acts of misconduct while previously members of Congress, the House implicitly denied it had jurisdiction over these cases. By initiating the investigation of Matteson, the House had at least approached the questions about the time and place of offenses and the possibility that it might have jurisdiction. But the failure to act, or act conclusively, in cases involving men reelected to Congress left the time and place questions unanswered. We should, therefore, compare what a chamber did when a member was charged with an act of misconduct that occurred before his reelection with what it did when a member was charged with an offense that occurred before he was first elected to Congress.

---

[30] 27 ibid. 304–311 (1858).
[31] The committee report and the views thereon are in ibid., pp. 1390–1391.

The Extra-Constitutional Questions between 1789 and 1860

Misconduct prior to a first-term election is only one issue in determining how each chamber came to define the boundaries of its powers. However, because such misconduct falls within the category of extra-constitutional questions and may be grounds for exclusion, we should discuss this issue in conjunction with others. We can therefore direct our attention to the Humphrey Marshall case of 1796, since it was the first to pose the question whether a chamber can judge a member's conduct before his election.

Allegations of wrongdoing were brought against Senator Marshall only after he had been seated, and referred to an incident that occurred eighteen months before his election. Inasmuch as a senate committee investigated the charges, at least to that extent the Senate claimed jurisdiction. But, we may ask, if the committee had discovered that Marshall was indeed guilty of "a gross fraud" and of perjury in a civil suit in a Kentucky court, would he have been subject to expulsion? Although the answer is uncertain (the committee reported that it had not been provided with evidence and records to substantiate the charges against Marshall), part of the committee's report, as amended and approved by the Senate 16 to 8, is critical to our understanding of early congressional attitudes toward the constitutional question. In part the report stated: "as the Constitution does not give jurisdiction to the Senate, the consent of the party [Marshall's later request for a complete investigation] cannot give it."[32] On this occasion the Senate disclaimed jurisdiction and thereby implied that a chamber may not enlarge upon the list of qualifications.

A decade later, the same position was taken by a House committee. At issue in the McCreery case (1807) was the question whether a state may prescribe additional qualifications, such as requiring that representatives reside in the districts from which they are elected. Representative Findley, chairman of the Committee on Elections, declared that the qualifications of members were "unalterably determined by the Federal Convention," that they can be affected only by constitutional amendment, and

---

[32] *Debates and Proceedings of the U.S. Congress*, 4th Congress, 1st sess., pp. 54–58 (1796), reel no. 2.

that "neither the State nor the Federal Legislatures are vested with authority to add to these qualifications, so as to change them."[33]

In each of these cases the chambers limited their power to judge a member-elect to specified constitutional grounds. And yet both the House and the Senate conducted inquiries into matters in no way related to age, citizenship, inhabitancy, or any of the several disqualifications prescribed in the Constitution. Although these investigations did not result in members-elect being denied seats in Congress, they permit us to raise a question. Let us suppose that committee investigations revealed an individual was guilty of prior misconduct or similar charges and that neither extenuating circumstances nor other considerations modified or offset the objections to his being seated. Would the House or Senate then claim that it did not have the power to act?

One illustration of the importance of this question is related to the dual charge brought against Philip Barton Key in 1808 after the inhabitancy issue was introduced—that he joined the British army after the signing of the Declaration of Independence and received half-pay as a British officer from 1783 through 1805. Upon investigation, the Committee on Elections determined that (1) his military service had been confined to expeditions against the Spanish in Florida, (2) there was no evidence that he had taken an oath of allegiance to the crown, and (3) his pay had been assigned to a destitute brother-in-law who was unable to provide for his family. By a narrow vote, Key's right to membership was sustained by the House.[34]

It is not possible to determine from the record whether the minority in the House vote objected to Key's seating because of the inhabitancy question, or the extra-constitutional issues, or both. John Randolph may have reflected the general attitude of the minority in warning against seating Key because of the inhabitance issue, claiming a dangerous precedent would be established. Wealthy and influential groups might arrange a few days' residence in a state to make their hand-picked candidates eligible for election as representatives. If all the negative votes were cast because of this possibility, the Key case suggests noth-

---

[33] Ibid., 10th Congress, 1st sess., p. 872 (1807), reel no. 4.
[34] Ibid., pp. 1489, 1680, 1849 (1808).

ing definitive about a chamber's adding to the qualifications of members-elect. Nevertheless, the extenuating circumstances in the case are important; otherwise a majority of the representatives might have declared him ineligible by reason of his service to England.[35]

Not until 1844, when Senator-elect John M. Niles of Connecticut appeared to take the oath of office, was a chamber again faced with the constitutional question. Niles, whose six-year term was to commence on March 4, 1844, had been ill and was unable to take the oath until April 30, although he had resided in the District of Columbia during the preceding weeks. After a story had circulated that he was mentally ill, Senator Jarnigan of Tennessee proposed that the oath not be administered until a select committee could report that Niles was competent to assume the duties of a senator.

Also, Jarnigan stated his belief that Niles would be disqualified by reason of this condition,[36] and thereby brought the constitutional question to the fore. In proposing the establishment of a select committee, he had suggested uncertainty about the Senate's ability to disqualify a man on grounds of mental incompetency: the committee should be established "if it be within [the Senate's] constitutional power to investigate the qualifications of Senators." Later in this statement, however, he said he believed the Senate had the necessary authority under the Constitution.[37]

The wording of Jarnigan's resolution is important. He proposed that the committee "be instructed to inquire into the election, returns, and qualifications" of Niles "and into his capacity" to take the oath. Senator Allen suggested that Jarnigan strike all reference to Niles's capacity since "qualifications" was comprehensive enough "to give general scope to the inquiry." The President pro tem, Senator Fairfield of Maine, also objected to the language of the resolution. The Senate, he argued, was not competent to undertake such an inquiry, "and it would be setting

---

[35] The matter of Key's pension evoked comments in the debate and was responsible for a proposal of Jan. 22, 1808, that a committee be established to consider the possibility of legislation "to punish any person, holding an office of profit or trust under the United States," who received money or accepted "gifts, emoluments, office or title from a foreign power" (ibid., p. 1495).

[36] 13 *Congressional Globe* 564 (1844).

[37] Ibid.

a very bad precedent, to authorize . . . an inquiry into the mental qualifications of senators."[38] Fairfield agreed that there should be an investigation, but only because of Niles's willingness and not because the Senate could claim constitutional authority. By adopting the Jarnigan rather than the Fairfield resolution, the Senate implied that it had ample authority to conduct an inquiry for reasons other than those specified in the Constitution.

When Jarnigan, chairman of the committee, submitted his report on May 16, 1844, he announced that the members were satisfied that the election, returns, and qualifications of Niles "were legal and sufficient." And medical testimony indicated that Niles was mentally sound. Therefore Niles was declared qualified and administered the oath of office.[39]

The Niles case, nevertheless, brought the legislators only to the threshold of the constitutional issue. Few senators had entered into discussion, and at no time had there been an explicit vote on the question: Does the Senate have the power to judge on grounds other than those prescribed in the Constitution? We cannot say, therefore, that the constitutional question was answered on this occasion. Yet we cannot overlook the fact that a new dimension had been introduced, for a Senate committee had inquired into the mental condition of a senator-elect. If the medical evidence had not been favorable, or if Niles had manifested mental quirks in his appearance before the committee, it is possible that the Senate would have voted to exclude him.

At least one new dimension of the constitutional issue was introduced when Representative Briggs of New York proposed an investigation into the election of the territorial delegate from Utah, John M. Bernhisel. In part, this demand grew out of reports of federal officers about corrupt practices in Utah, but Briggs alluded also to the possibility of bribery and corruption by Brigham Young and Bernhisel to bring about the latter's election.[40] Since each house is explicitly empowered to judge the election and the returns of its members, a congressional inquiry would have been authorized by the Constitution, but when various members objected to this resolution, claiming that the charges against Bernhisel were based upon rumors, Briggs with-

---

[38] Ibid.
[39] Ibid., p. 602.
[40] 21 *Congressional Globe* 306 (1852).

drew it. Neverthelsss, he had created a situation wherein members of the House could consider the breadth of their power.

Representative Cartter of Ohio believed that the investigation should be made—and that, in addition, it should determine whether polygamy was practiced in the territory and whether Bernhisel was a polygamist. When one of his colleagues called out "what if he is?" Cartter answered that he would vote for expelling a polygamist from the chamber: "I will not consent silently to sit upon this floor with any man who openly defies the laws of his country as a polygamist."[41]

Although no one asked whether it was possible for the House to exclude a polygamist, Cartter's reaction anticipated an attitude that would gain increasing support over the next decade and more, as the Nebraska Bill, the situation in "Bleeding" Kansas, the rise of the Republican Party, *Dred Scott*, the hatreds engendered by slavery, and secession divided the nation. Yet these events also contributed to the emergence of a definitive answer to the constitutional question, and the case of Senator Trumbull of Illinois set the stage for the actions of the House and the Senate in the next phase.

At issue was a provision of the Illinois constitution of 1848 that barred state judges from election to other state and national offices during the term of their judgeships and for one year thereafter. Other state constitutions of that day contained similar provisions; indeed, some senators said that they or various colleagues were presently in violation of their state constitutions. They therefore reported that, as their rights to membership had not been challenged, Trumbull's claim to a Senate seat was opposed for partisan reasons.

Trumbull had been elected to a nine-year state judicial post in 1852 but had resigned his judgeship in 1854, about eighteen months before his election to the Senate. At least two major questions are germane to this case. First, may a state impose a requirement that temporarily disqualifies a man for national office? Second, if a state may impose such a condition, did it operate in Trumbull's case, since he had resigned the judgeship more than a year before his election to the Senate?

Although different views were expressed in the debate, those of

---

[41] Ibid., p. 354.

Senator Butler of South Carolina had the greatest relevance, and within a few years represented the position subscribed to by most members of Congress. To Butler, the situation was so clear that it removed all doubt about the Senate's power. Suppose, he said, a state legislature were to send a convict, who met the age, citizenship, and inhabitancy requirements to the Senate. Must the Senate seat him?

I say no; because I resort to another article of the Constitution to protect the Senate—the clause allowing it to expel a member. I would expel him at once. Gentlemen may ask, how expel him? Would you give him a seat and then turn him out? No sir; if a man comes to my door, who I think is a scoundrel, I will kick him away at once, and not allow him to come in and then kick him out.[42]

In 1858, support for this position was implicit in a proposal by Senator Harlan and explicit in a statement by Senator Jefferson Davis of Mississippi. After Minnesota was admitted to statehood, and one of its Senators-elect, Henry M. Rice, presented his credentials, an objection was voiced by Harlan, who said that Rice, as land agent for the Department of the Army, had defrauded settlers on the Fort Crawford Reservation in Iowa. Jefferson Davis contended that if Harlan "considered the accusation such as disqualified [Rice] for a seat, the Senate being the judge of the qualifications of its members, he had a right to raise the question" before the oath of office was administered.[43]

The debate, however, did not turn upon the merits of Davis's claim. Various senators were more concerned about protecting Rice from calumny and criticizing Harlan for his tactics than in claiming a broad power to judge the qualifications of a member-elect. Harlan should have informed Rice in advance that objections would be made to the latter's being given the oath of office, they argued; he should not have waited until this moment to present the charges. Rice was given the oath, and although both he and Harlan introduced resolutions calling for an investigation of the charges by a select committee, no action was taken on either proposal.

It is noteworthy that in 1856 and 1858 the pro-slavery, states' rights–oriented senators from South Carolina and Mississippi

---

[42] 25 *Congressional Globe* 547 (1856).
[43] 27 ibid., 2075–2079 (1858).

argued in favor of a broad discretionary power to judge the qualifications of members-elect and that shortly thereafter this same argument was voiced by an abolitionist, Senator Sumner of Massachusetts. Now, however, the undesirables who might be sent to the Senate by a state legislature were not "convicts" but the "traitors" who led the slaveholding states out of the Union.

IV

Initial Answers to the Constitutional Questions:
Loyalty, the Civil War, and Reconstruction

Overview of the Situation between 1861 and 1871

Secession and the Civil War answered the constitutional question exactly as Senators Butler and Davis had claimed it should be answered: A chamber may judge a member-elect on grounds other than those stipulated in the Constitution. Although the principal issue had been loyalty to the Union, the answer that was formulated during the Civil War and Reconstruction made it easier for each chamber to dispose of other cases on extra-constitutional grounds. Between 1860 and 1900, various issues—loyalty, corruption, polygamy, and misconduct, whether before election or reelection—permitted the House and the Senate to go far beyond the earlier cases and extend their power to judge both qualifications and conduct in ways they had not contemplated prior to the Civil War.

In examining the Civil War and Reconstruction cases we must, of course, be aware of the political context within which answers to constitutional questions were given and standards were applied. Because the disposition of cases was often dictated by political considerations, an answer in any specific case might only appear to have had constitutional sanction. In fact, however, many cases were so impacted by political factors that the transparency of their answers soon becomes obvious. Keeping all this in mind, we must nevertheless acknowledge the signficance of politically impacted decisions for changing and defining the limits of congressional power. No matter how imperfect the analogies with precedents or how inconsistent the application of standards, the Civil War period produced important developments with respect to the power of each house to judge the qualifications and conduct of its members. These developments will command our attention in this and later chapters.

Within a single decade, 1861 to 1871, members-elect were judged on both constitutional and extra-constitutional grounds. Moreover, Congress added still another dimension to the constitutional question by using its *legislative* power to exclude certain persons from office—more, that is, than the specific constitutional requirements of age, citizenship, and inhabitancy. Also, important questions about a second office, and a state's republican form of government, together with extra-constitutional qualifications, were asked more frequently as subjects for congressional consideration. The extent and diversity of such issues, and of course their disposition, led to each chamber's defining its powers more broadly than it had in the past. In 1862, Congress used its legislative power and the oath requirement of the Constitution in enacting the Oath of Office Act. Finally, Congress added a new constitutional disqualification in the disability section (Sec. 3) of the Fourteenth Amendment.[1]

The cases that were decided during the Civil War and Reconstruction were seldom limited to the single issue of whether a member-elect fulfilled a constitutional or extra-constitutional requirement. For example, a case that centered on inhabitancy could be complicated by such matters as violence and corruption attending an election. Or there might be a question whether the agency that issued a certificate of election was a recognizable

---

[1] "No person shall be a Senator or Representative . . . who, having previously taken an oath, as a member of Congress, or as an officer of the United States, or as a member of any State legislature, or as an executive or judicial officer of any State, to support the Constitution of the United States, shall have engaged in insurrection or rebellion against the same, or given aid or comfort to the enemies thereof. But Congress may, by a vote of two-thirds of each House, remove such disability."

authority, whether an election had been decided by the votes of people within the "pacified" area of a congressional district, and whether a state had a republican form of government (whether, that is, it had been "reconstructed" to the satisfaction of the Radicals who controlled Congress).

These matters, nonetheless, were directly related to the constitutional question about the right of a state and its people to be represented in Congress. Since, as was frequently claimed during the war, a state may not secede from the Union, it follows that its right to be represented in Congress may not be abridged. But, for various reasons people within secessionist states were denied this right to representation.

One of the problems derived from uncertainty about who had the authority to conduct elections and issue a certificate of election within a secessionist state. There had been no problem in the few cases in which Unionists had remained in Congress after their states had seceded; however, once a secessionist vacancy occurred, there were doubts as to the validity of the credentials presented by a nonsecessionist member-elect. The uncertainty of the House and the Senate about the proper procedure for filling vacancies was shown in two cases that involved John E. Segar, a Unionist from Virginia. Questioning the validity of his credentials, the House refused to admit him on February 11, 1862, but later, on May 6, 1862, it decided not to question the authority of the agency that had issued his certificate of election, and it voted to seat Segar. Segar's pro-Union sympathies were no doubt responsible for the latter decision. Yet, in 1865, Segar's patriotism did not preclude the Senate's concern about the validity of his credentials. From all reports, Charles Sumner announced, Segar had been appointed to a Senate seat by the common council of the city of Alexandria—to the seat that had become vacant upon the death of another Unionist from Virginia, Senator Bowden. In denying membership to Segar the Senate agreed that the common council of Alexandria was not a state agency and did not have the authority to issue a certificate of election.[2]

Two broad categories of cases arose in the years between 1861 and 1871: one involved the question about a state having earned the right to be represented in Congress; the other pertained to

---

[2] 35 *Congressional Globe* 845–846 (1865).

the rights of individual members-elect. With respect to the first category, and over a period of several years, the Radical-controlled Congress redefined the right of states of the Confederacy to be represented in the national legislature. By a joint resolution in July 1866, Tennessee was readmitted to Congress. In 1868, representatives and senators from Alabama, Arkansas, Florida, Louisiana, North Carolina, and South Carolina were seated. Although six representatives-elect from Georgia were seated in 1868, the state was denied membership in the Senate until 1870. Only in 1870 were Texas, Virginia, and Mississippi readmitted.

Cases in the second category require individual attention rather than blanket summary because of the many different kinds of situations that arose during the Civil War and Reconstruction. Some cases involved the specific constitutional requirements; others raised questions about a chamber's power to judge the qualifications and conduct of members and members-elect; and various cases are distinguishable in that their disposition was exclusion, expulsion, or censure. And yet, since the issue of loyalty to the Union was the central focal point, there was the possibility that the House or Senate might analogize from one case to another, thereby creating usable precedents. This tendency was reflected in a statement by Senator Sumner on January 6, 1862, when a question was raised about the eligibility of Benjamin Stark of Oregon:

The Senate is at this moment engaged in considering the loyalty of certain members of this body, and it seems to me it would poorly do its duty if it admitted among its members one with regard to whom, as he came forth to take the oath, there was a reasonable suspicion.[3]

The relevance of this claim will become more apparent as we look at the instances in which the Senate acted to expel sitting members.

Confederates, Sympathizers, and Suspects

As states seceded from the Union their representatives and senators withdrew from Congress. Thus on several occasions in 1861 each house declared these seats vacant and expelled men

---

[3] 32 ibid., 184 (1862).

who were no longer present; and their expulsion was largely a quixotic gesture. Also, because they were serving the Confederacy at that time, Breckinridge of Kentucky and Johnson and Polk of Missouri were expelled in late 1861 and early 1862. But movements to expel or to censure members who were still present and the attempt to deny membership to Stark were of much greater significance.

There can be no doubt that each house has the power to define an act of misconduct by a sitting member and provide for his punishment. Thus the Senate felt justified in expelling Jesse Bright of Indiana for giving a gun salesman a letter of introduction to President Jefferson Davis. Mr. Thomas B. Lincoln, Bright wrote, has an idea for "a great improvement in firearms." This letter, dated March 1, 1861, and given to Lincoln at a time when war was imminent, Senator Morton S. Wilkinson of Minnesota argued, was evidence of disloyalty to the United States and justification for Bright's expulsion from the Senate. Friends and various colleagues of Bright argued that hostilities had not commenced at the time the letter was written and that the incident should therefore be considered nothing more than an act of friendship whereby the writer sought to introduce one acquaintance to another for the purpose of transacting business.[4] Neither these arguments nor the claim that Bright was being railroaded for purely partisan reasons had any effect. He was expelled on February 5, 1862, by a vote of 32 to 14.

The Senate also directed special attention to the actions and statements of Senator Lazarus Powell of Kentucky, who on two occasions in 1861 attended "States' rights" conventions. These conventions had adopted resolutions that condemned the national government, and they were attended by "most intense secessionists" whose speeches were "fraught with the frankest treason." For these reasons Senator Wilkinson proposed (on February 19, 1862) that Powell be expelled. Even the General Assembly of Kentucky was in favor of Powell's expulsion.

After a Senate committee investigated the charges, it stated that Powell had done no more than express the neutralist sentiment of the people of Kentucky, which contradicted the state-

---

[4] Ibid., p. 391.

ment of Senator Davis.[5] The committee also distinguished between Powell's conduct and Breckinridge's: the latter had become an officer in the Confederate Army, whereas Powell returned to the Senate to discharge his duties. As a final justification for opposing his expulsion, the committee recommended that a senator not be punished for expressing opinions. The committee's findings and recommendations were accepted by the Senate, and the resolution to expel was defeated 28 to 11.[6]

It was with reference to these expulsion cases that Senator Sumner proposed the exclusion of Benjamin Stark of Oregon. Stark had received an interim appointment from the governor, the Oregon legislature not being in session at the time a vacancy occurred. Since this was a question of exclusion rather than expulsion, and was based upon matters that had no direct relationship to constitutional qualifications, it presented the issue of whether a chamber may judge its members on broader grounds.

Affidavits from residents of Oregon challenged Stark's right to be a senator. He was, they claimed, "an open and avowed supporter of secession." Furthermore, they contended, Stark had publicly announced that, in the event of a civil war, he would move to the South and join the rebels. Since these statements, if true, had been made prior to Stark's appointment to the Senate, could the Senate exclude him? Initially, Senator William P. Fessenden of Maine argued that "Mr. Stark should not be admitted to a seat" if the allegations were proved.[7] He later modified this, claiming he meant that Stark should be given the oath of office and then, if the charges were proved, should be expelled.[8] Even as modified, Fessenden's statement introduced the same constitutional question: May a chamber expel a member whose misconduct occurred prior to his election?

The other constitutional issue was introduced by Sumner, who said the Senate would not be doing its duty if it admitted Stark at the very moment it was considering expelling members for disloyal utterances or actions. Admittedly, Sumner told his col-

---

[5] Davis had read from a resolution of the Kentucky General Assembly, adopted in Nov. 1861, requesting that both Senators Breckinridge and Powell *resign* since they no longer represented the will of the people (32 *Congressional Globe* 1209 [1862]).

[6] Ibid., p. 1230.

[7] Ibid., p. 183.

[8] Remarks of Feb. 18, 1862, in ibid., p. 869.

leagues, there was no precedent upon which the Senate could call. "It belongs, therefore, to the Senate to make a precedent in order to deal with an unprecedented case."[9] The opposite viewpoint was voiced by Senator Bayard: "No matter how debased his moral character might be, no matter though he lie under the stigma of an indictment and conviction for a crime," a member-elect who presents valid credentials must be given the oath of office.[10] This was "a monstrous doctrine," Senator Trumbull of Illinois retorted; surely the Senate would not accept the credentials of Jefferson Davis and other traitors whose purpose in seeking membership was "to set fire to the powder that is to blow up the Capitol."

Although Stark was seated, we can not claim that Bayard's view had prevailed over Sumner's. A number of senators were troubled by the fact that the allegations against Stark were unsubstantiated and appeared to be no more than rumors obtained through *ex parte* proceedings. This in itself constituted a serious procedural deficiency. And, as Senator Fessenden commented in modifying his position, there was also the fact that other men who, in the heat of debate, had made statements as serious as Stark's were now fighting in the Union forces.[11] For one or more reasons—doubt about the power of the Senate or uncertainty over the truth of the allegations—the Senate accepted its committee's majority report that Stark was "entitled to take the constitutional oath of office."[12] On February 27 he was given the oath "without prejudice to any further proceedings in this case."

Further investigation of the charges was made by a select committee (initiated at the request of Stark), and in late April it reported that Stark was not loyal to the United States. After several weeks, when Sumner asked the committee chairman when he was going to seek Senate action on the report, the chairman answered that his committee had fulfilled its responsibility under

[9] Ibid., p. 184.

[10] Ibid., p. 265.

[11] Ibid., p. 869.

[12] Report of the committee (Feb. 7, 1862), ibid., p. 696. Only Senator Trumbull dissented. In his minority report he argued that the Senate was competent "to go beyond these questions, and to ascertain what had been the conduct and deportment of the candidate for a seat in the Senate even before his election or appointment" (ibid., p. 861).

the resolution by conducting an inquiry and making a report. Another member of the committee proposed that no more of the Senate's time be devoted to the case. Because Stark's short-term appointment would soon end, he said, the people of Oregon could make the decision. Dissatisfied with these answers, Sumner proposed that Stark be expelled, but his resolution was defeated 21 to 16.[13]

Neither constitutional question—neither the one posed by Fessenden in his claim that Stark should be seated and then expelled if the charges against him were proved true nor the one posed by Sumner in his request that the Senate create a precedent by excluding Stark—was answered on this occasion. For various reasons, such as unsubstantiated rumors, *ex parte* proceedings, a question about the extent of senatorial power, and the likelihood that the Oregon legislature would dispose of Stark, senators had not felt compelled to answer the constitutional questions.

Although the Sumner forces suffered defeat in the Stark case, they could take comfort from a development in July 1862: the passage of the test-oath law. During the debates in the Stark case, Sumner had argued that the oath required by Article VI, clause 3 is required of members of Congress as much as the qualifications of age, citizenship, and inhabitancy, and by enacting the Oath of Office Bill in July 1862 Congress implicitly agreed. Previously all members-elect had rendered a positive statement of support for the Constitution of the United States. But now, under the Act of 1862, they had to render a disclaimer against having (1) borne arms against the United States, (2) sought or served in an office under the authority of a government hostile to the United States, and (3) aided, counseled, or countenanced enemies of the United States.[14] This act was to become a powerful weapon in the hands of the Radicals, one which they could use as the political situation indicated.

One of the committee recommendations in the case of Senator Powell of Kentucky—that no member of congress be punished for expressing opinions—was in the spirit though not the form of the constitutional provision that "for any speech or debate in

---

[13] The resolution was defeated June 6, 1862. Prior to the convening of the next Congress, the Oregon legislator chose a senator other than Stark, thereby rendering the decision most senators seemed to expect.

[14] 12 *United States Statutes at Large* 502 (1863).

either house (senators and representatives) shall not be questioned in any other place."[15] "Legislators have an obligation to take positions on controversial public questions," declared Chief Justice Warren in the *Bond* case, for only then can their constituents "be fully informed by them, and be better able to assess their qualifications for office."[16] But exercise of this right of expression was undermined on three counts in 1864, when legislators became the targets of either expulsion or censure moves by reason of their comments on the Confederacy, the Civil War, or the Lincoln Administration.

Garrett Davis of Kentucky, who had been a prominent figure in the effort to have Lazarus Powell expelled from the Senate, soon became the object of a similar effort and resolution. On January 5, 1864, Davis had made a statement about Northerners bringing an end to the war by taking matters into their own hands. The intention of this remark, Senator Henry Wilson claimed, was to incite a revolt against constitutional authority, and because of such treasonable conduct, Davis should be expelled.[17] Incitement to rebellion was not his purpose, Davis answered; rather, he wanted the people of the North and the South, acting through established political channels, to seek the policies necessary for ending the war. A letter from Davis to the chairman of the Committee on Military Affairs disavowed any intent of action outside the political system. On January 27 the Senate turned its attention to the possibility of censuring rather than expelling Davis.

While the intent of Davis's proposals remained central to the ensuing debates, there was vigorous advocacy of the right to discuss such matters freely. Some senators argued that exercise of the right of freedom of expression should not invite threats of expulsion or censure, and their arguments seem to have been accepted. Although there were many adverse comments about what Davis had said and about his intent, the decision was reached on January 28 to withdraw the resolution to expel him.[18]

---

[15] Article I, sec. 6 (1).

[16] Bond v. Floyd, 87 S. Ct. 339, 349 (1966).

[17] A series of resolutions proposed by Davis is found at 34 *Congressional Globe* 96–97 (1864). Wilson's resolution to expel Davis was introduced Jan. 8 (ibid., p. 139).

[18] Ibid., p. 394.

Representatives Alexander Long of Ohio and Benjamin G. Harris of Maryland in 1864, Fernando Wood of New York in 1868, and John Young Brown of Kentucky in 1875 were not as successful in maintaining their claims to the right of freedom of expression and dissent. The earliest cases, arising in the third year of the Civil War, were necessarily more impacted by events than the two cases that arose in 1868 and 1875. Nevertheless, the Radicals' reaction to dissenting opinions was not markedly different on any of these occasions, which suggests that circumstances need not be of the nature Justice Holmes considered necessary before the clear and present danger doctrine may be employed.

In the words of Schuyler Colfax of Indiana, Representative Long had "declared himself in favor of recognizing the independence and nationality of the so-called confederacy." Such a declaration, said Colfax, gave aid and comfort to the enemies of the United States; therefore Long should be expelled.[19] But at the outset of this speech Long had announced his intention "to indulge in that freedom of speech and latitude of debate" permitted by both the rules of the House and the Constitution. That the Radicals were seriously disturbed by Long's comments, and did not acknowledge the right to dissent, was demonstrated by the fact that Colfax, Speaker of the House, introduced the resolution demanding Long's expulsion. The Long affair lasted from April 9 to April 14.

On the other hand, Benjamin Harris, who made comments that led to his censure in the course of the Long debate, found himself in immediate danger of punishment. In a lengthy speech, Harris, a self-proclaimed "radical peace man," had pleaded for recognition of the Confederacy, saying the South wanted only to live in peace, which was something the North would not permit. "God Almighty grant that . . . you will never subjugate the South."[20] Apparently his comments were regarded as even more dangerous than Long's, for a resolution to expel Harris was introduced and voted on that same day. The expulsion of Harris failed to carry because of the two-thirds requirement (81 to 58), but the vote

---

[19] 34 *Congressional Globe* 1515 (1864).
[20] Ibid., p. 1516.

was substantial enough to lead immediately to a censure resolution, which was adopted, 93 to 18.[21]

The decision in the Long case was not reached until April 14, 1864, five days after the expulsion resolution was introduced. Because the Radicals knew that they could not get the two-thirds vote needed to expel, they now sought to censure Long. The members should not lose sight of free speech, which is an important element in a body representing different views and opinions, Representative Eldridge of Wisconsin warned, but it was obvious that the Radicals believed Long had gone beyond permissible limits in his remarks almost a week earlier, for he was censured. His statements, the resolution declared, were evidence of disloyalty and signified infidelity to his oath as a member of Congress. He was, therefore, declared "to be an unworthy member of the House of Representatives."[22]

Even after the Civil War the Radicals sharply limited the comments of various members of Congress. While debating a Reconstruction bill, Representative Wood of New York called it "the most infamous of the many infamous acts of this infamous Congress."[23] This statement produced not only a vote to prohibit his further speaking on that occasion but a censure resolution. By 114 to 39 the House adopted the resolution, introduced by Representative Dawes of Massachusetts.

Dawes also gained prominence several years later when he sought the expulsion of John Young Brown of Kentucky. The Civil Rights Bill of 1875, Brown had declared, was another part of the Radicals' scheme to deny the South constitutional liberties and harass the broken land.[24] Because, it was alleged, Brown's comments were intended to deceive the American people, a resolution to censure him was introduced. But Brown's comments, Lucius Lamar of Mississippi countered, were no more serious than those of others. There was, for example, Hale's likening of a colleague to a "dirty dog" and Butler's reference to Bingham of Ohio as a judge who presided over "a judicial murder upon insufficient evidence." No one had proposed that either man be

---

[21] Ibid., p. 1518.
[22] Ibid., p. 1634.
[23] 39 *Congressional Globe* 541 (1868).
[24] 3 *Congressional Record* 986 (1875).

censured or expelled for such statements, Lamar argued. Dawes, though admitting these incidents, said that "errors we committed heretofore do not justify our present errors."[25] To atone for "present errors," Dawes favored Brown's expulsion, but knowing that he did not have the necessary two-thirds vote to expel, he had to be satisfied with a censure resolution, which was adopted February 4, 1875.[26]

Constitutional Requirements and the Civil War

John Young Brown, who previous to his censure had been excluded from membership by reason of disability under the Test Oath Act of 1862, was less than twenty-five years of age when he was first elected to Congress.[27] It had not been necessary for the House to decide at what moment a member-elect must meet the constitutional requirements since Brown's political disability was ground enough for his exclusion.[28] This was the only instance in which the constitutional age factor might have been raised between 1860 and 1900. Other constitutional qualifications—citizenship, inhabitancy, and the second-office provision—were of greater consequence during the Civil war, as in the case of Charles Upton, a representative from Virginia, who was challenged in July 1861.

By his own admission, Upton had voted in Ohio, yet he claimed to be a resident of Virginia. Although the Committee on Elections found him to be an inhabitant of Virginia, in February 1862 it reported that he was not entitled to membership. New issues had been introduced into his case—questions about the validity of his election that grew out of the confusion created by Virginia's secession from the Union and reports that force and violence had been used to prevent some citizens from voting. By

---

[25] Ibid., p. 990.

[26] Ibid. Fifteen months later Lamar succeeded in having certain portions of the censure resolution expunged, although the stigma of censure was not removed thereby (4 *Congressional Record* 2887–2888, [May 2, 1876]).

[27] This information was reported in 1875 by Representative Dawes. Brown resided in the District of Columbia, said Dawes, "waiting his arrival at a constitutional majority" (3 *Congressional Record* 987 [1875]).

[28] This occurred in 1867. We will consider it in the next section of this chapter in conjunction with other incidents.

an unrecorded vote, Upton was declared ineligible for membership in the House.[29]

Jennings Pigott, a "carpetbagger" in North Carolina, was denied membership in the House in 1863. Inhabitancy was not the only issue in this case, for he was elected from a congressional district in which the residents of only three of the eleven counties had voted. The remainder of the district was under rebel control, the Committee on Elections reported, and even within the three counties guerrilla action had made voter participation difficult. The committee's report stated that Pigott could not "be deemed the choice of the loyal voters of the district in which more than half of them had no opportunity to express that choice."[30] But Representative Clements argued that rebel activity should not be permitted to deprive loyal citizens of enjoying their constitutional rights, and loyal citizens, he added, had chosen Pigott to be their representative in Congress.

For his part, Pigott declared that although he had resided within the District of Columbia for about ten years before the war, he had always intended to return to his native state, North Carolina. He said he had been appointed to "an office in North Carolina in the fall of 1861" but circumstances delayed his moving there. When he at last returned home, it was as secretary to the United States military governor. "I always told the people that I was going back home," Pigott declared,

and I always looked forward to the day when I should return to my native home in North Carolina, God bless the old state of North Carolina—a state in which I would rather live than any place on the face of the earth.[31]

Neither Clements's nor Pigott's arguments had the desired effect, for the House accepted the committee's resolution that Pigott was not entitled to membership. Although the reasons stated for this decision appear to be convincing, they are in sharp

---

[29] Upton had been seated when the House refused to accept a resolution declaring him ineligible, but this resolution was based solely upon the inhabitancy question. The other issues, later brought to light by the committee, were responsible for his being unseated, not expelled. This meant, then, that his claim to membership was invalid from the beginning. (31 *Congressional Globe* 3 [1861] and 32 ibid., 1010 [1862]).

[30] 33 ibid., 1209 (1863).

[31] Ibid.

contrast to those in other instances of violence and voter intimidation. There were few refusals to seat similar members-elect; indeed another "carpetbagger," Adelbert Ames, was seated as a senator from Mississippi.

In many cases a House or Senate committee had to investigate a number of charges, not just one, and therefore such cases were not affected solely by partisan attitudes. A typical case was the contested election between Simon Jones and James Mann of Louisiana, which began with charges of voter intimidation and a failure to meet the inhabitancy requirements—a case that soon involved two other principals, J. W. Menard, a black, and Caleb Hunt. The dispute began in December 1868, when Jones claimed he was entitled to the seat that had been given to Mann.

Jones made three charges. First, his supporters had been kept away from the polls by violence and intimidation. Second, there was evidence of "ballot-box stuffing." And third, Mann could not validly claim to be an inhabitant of Louisiana.[32] Mann was seated in July 1868 but had died the following month, and a special election was called for the vacant seat. Jones, who claimed this seat for the foregoing reasons, had not entered the second election, in which both Menard and Hunt claimed victory. Thus the House was faced with two questions: (1) Did the seat rightfully belong to Jones? (2) If Jones was declared ineligible, which of the other two men should be seated?

Jones's claim was dismissed after a committee reported, that, though there was evidence of fraud in the first election, not more than 100 votes were involved. Since Mann's plurality had been 1,150 votes, the election's outcome was unaffected by the 100 fraudulent votes. With respect to inhabitancy, the committee's statement indicated there was "nothing clear or satisfactory; nothing that would justify the committee in deciding that Mr. Mann was ineligible as a candidate at the time of the election."[33] On February 27, 1869, the House declared that Jones was not entitled to membership, because he had not received a majority of the votes. The members then directed their attention to the Menard-Hunt contest.

House Democrats apparently were pleased with these develop-

[32] 40 *Congressional Globe* 15 (1869).
[33] Ibid., p. 1679.

ments, because they might force the Republican majority into the position of denying membership to a Negro, Menard, who held the certificate of election. Why, asked Democratic Representative Ross, did his "political friends" not seat him? Would Menard "not have his rights like any other citizen because of his race or color?"[34]

At issue was the "carpetbaggers' " invalidation of more than 19,000 votes of the 27,000 total. The votes of only three of seven parishes (counties) were counted by the committee of canvassers, and Hunt's total was reduced by 11,535 because the canvassers invalidated the votes of Orleans Parish. Within the four parishes not counted, Hunt had 14,368 and Menard 5,201 votes. There was every indication that the election had been conducted in compliance with state law; nevertheless, a proposal to seat Hunt was defeated 137 to 41, and by a 130 to 57 vote the House denied membership to Menard. It then recommitted the matter to the committee for investigation to determine the validity of the election and whether violence and disorder had made it impossible to hold an election that was fair and free.[35]

The Menard case did not consider whether Menard met the citizenship requirement, but this requirement was to become an issue in the Senate the following year, when another Negro, Hiram Revels, appeared as a member-elect from Mississippi. The initial objection to Revels was the fact that his credentials were signed by Brevet Major General Adelbert Ames, the "carpetbagger" provisional governor of Mississippi and the claimant to Mississippi's other seat in the United States Senate. But a provisional governor was not a governor within the meaning of the law, Democratic Senators Saulsbury, Davis, and Stockton contended. However, there were precedents for seating Revels in that the credentials of the two senators from Virginia had been signed by a provisional governor and had been accepted.[36] But this was more than a technical question, claimed Senator Edmunds, inasmuch as those who objected to Revels had other motives. There could be little doubt of the implication in his statement, for—as

---

[34] Ibid., p. 1683.
[35] Ibid., p. 1696.
[36] Exchanges on this issue are found in 42 *Congressional Globe* 1503–1504 (1870).

Senator Davis soon made very clear—the racial issue was upper-most.

Revels presented his credentials approximately one year after Menard had sought admission to the House of Representatives, yet Senator Davis, introducing the race issue, claimed that this was the first time a black man had presented himself before either chamber. But if several *had* been elected to the House of Representatives, why had none of them appeared for admission? Davis offered an answer: "for a very plain reason; the members of the House who would vote for the reception of colored men have soon to return to the people to be passed upon at an election." Members of the Senate, on the other hand, could feel safer in admitting a Negro, since their terms of office would not expire until after the next election.[37]

However, the racial question, though significant, was not as important as whether Revels was a citizen of the United States. There were two reasons, Davis argued, why Revels could not claim citizenship: (1) Congress may provide only for the natur-alization of persons of foreign birth, not of those who were born within the jurisdiction of the United States; and (2) the *Dred Scott* decision showed that Revels was not a citizen. "He is not a citizen by one of the most learned, argumentative, powerful, and conclusive opinions that was ever written upon the bench."[38] There seems to be no justification for his first point, but impor-tant questions were posed by the *Dred Scott* decision of 1857 and its relationship to the Civil Rights Act of 1866 and the opening statement in the Fourteenth Amendment.

Davis felt there was ample support for his argument because, prior to the Civil War, free Negroes in both the North and the South had been denied the full rights of citizenship. Nominally free men, they had been denied the voting privilege in some states, freedom of mobility, the right to pursue certain occupa-

---

[37] Ibid., p. 1510. What Davis meant, of course, was that Representa-tives serve two-year terms while Senators serve for six years, conse-quently the former must face the voters more frequently.

[38] Ibid. The opening statement of the Fourteenth Amendment, adopted two years before the Revels case arose, would appear to dispose of the first claim. And by conferring citizenship upon Puerto Ricans, Aleuts, Eskimos, Indians, Guamanians, and Virgin Islanders between 1917 and 1950, Congress gave every indication that it was exercising the preroga-tive inherent in any sovereign state.

tions, and the right to marry whites. The state constitutions of Indiana, Illinois, Kansas, and Oregon even prohibited free black men from entering these states for the purpose of taking up residence.

There was, then, a question whether the Supreme Court's denial in *Dred Scott* that blacks were American citizens was an acknowledgment of conditions as they existed in much of the nation in 1857. On the other hand, the Civil Rights Act of 1866 declared:

That all persons of African descent born in the United States are hereby declared to be citizens of the United States, and there shall be no discrimination in civil rights or immunities among the inhabitants of any State or Territory of the United States on account of race, color, or previous condition of slavery.

And section 1 of the Fourteenth Amendment provides that "all persons born or naturalized in the United States and subject to the jurisdiction thereof, are citizens of the United States." Obviously, these statutory and constitutional provisions override *Dred Scott.* The question, therefore, is whether citizenship for Negroes was thereby confirmed as their birthright or whether the statute and the amendment conferred citizenship upon them as of the date of enactment and adoption. If the former was the case, Revels met the citizenship requirement. If, however, he could claim citizenship only from the moment the Civil Rights Bill was enacted (in 1866) or the Fourteenth Amendment was adopted (in 1868), he did not meet the constitutional requirement that a person must have been a citizen of the United States for nine years before he is eligible to become a senator.

Speaking to this issue on February 24, 1870, Senator Jacob Howard of Michigan expressed what was apparently the sentiment of most of his colleagues:

But I hold that in the sense of the Constitution every person born free within the limits of a State, not connected with a foreign minister's family, is born a citizen of the United States, whether he be white or black. Nativity imparts citizenship in all countries; and that is sufficient for my purpose. I carry this doctrine without hesitation so far as to assert that even a black man born a slave shall, so far as citizenship in this country, be held to have been a citizen from his birth.[39]

---

[39] Ibid., p. 1543.

By its vote to seat Revels (48 to 8),[40] the vast majority of the Senate implied support for the position stated by Howard, and thus section 1 of the Fourteenth Amendment could be regarded as enunciating a principle of long standing. This enunciation was necessary not to overturn the Supreme Court's decision on the citizenship issue, as though what it said was a fact, but because the statement was inconsistent with the principle that blacks possess citizenship as a birthright.

Only after the disposition of the Revels case did the Senate turn to Adelbert Ames, the provisional governor of Mississippi who had signed his own credentials for his election to an unexpired Senate term that commenced March 4, 1869. According to the report of the Committee on the Judiciary, Ames was a native of Maine, a graduate of West Point, and a general. Ames declared, however, that he had resigned his commission even before the President signed the bill that readmitted Mississippi to representation in Congress. He was, nevertheless, provisional governor of Mississippi at the time his name was submitted as a candidate for the Senate in January 1870, and shortly before the election he had announced his intention of becoming a resident of Mississippi. Given these facts, the Committee concluded that Ames was not an inhabitant at the time of his election; therefore he was not entitled to take the oath of office.[41]

The debate that followed the report of the committee focused on questions of inhabitancy and whether Ames's decision to resign his commission and his declaration of his intent to remain in Mississippi were adequate bases for inhabitancy within the meaning of the Constitution. As in the Revels case, the Radicals found ample support for a resolution that declared Ames was eligible.[42]

We might ask whether there was any need for either side to have entered into debate inasmuch as the important constitutional questions about inhabitancy and a second office were quickly disposed of with the seating of Ames. The debate and its

---

[40] A resolution to submit the issue to the Committee on the Judiciary was defeated by an identical vote, 48 to 8. The Senate then voted to seat Revels, on Feb. 25, 1870 (ibid., p. 1568).

[41] The committee report is found in ibid., p. 2052 (Mar. 18, 1870).

[42] A resolution by Senator Sumner that declared Ames eligible for membership was adopted by a vote of 40 to 12 on Apr. 1, 1870.

outcome provided no definitive answers to either question, almost wholly ignoring the time factor in constitutional qualification. It was apparent from the outset that the Republicans had the necessary votes, even though two prominent members of the party, Conkling and Trumbull, voted against Sumner's resolution to seat Ames. And despite his negative vote, Conkling had reported consoling news on March 22, 1870: since the January election, Ames had "qualified himself to be the eligible recipient of a fresh appointment." "The committee," he said, also was relieved "to know of the alacrity with which the Legislature of Mississippi will return him, thus removing from his way all challenge or exception."[43]

But how can we reconcile the Senate's seating of Ames and the House's denial of Pigott's claim to membership? True, there were distinguishing features in the Pigott case: less than half of his congressional district had been under Northern control, and, even within the three counties whose polls were open, guerrilla activities had hampered voting. However, it is appropriate to note the apparent contradictions in these and other cases, especially in the questions raised about holding a second office.

When the Committee on Elections recommended that Colonels Baker and Yell be declared disqualified for membership during the Mexican War, it had not distinguished between commissions in state volunteer units (which these men held) and commissions in the Army of the United States. Later, some members of the House believed that such a distinction should be made, but they were at least partially motivated by the fact that a "copperhead," Clement L. Vallandigham, had questioned the right of several representatives to be both members of Congress and commissioned officers in their state volunteer units. Indeed, Representative McKnight suggested that a committee determine whether Vallandigham "is accredited to this, or another *Congress*." On July 12, 1861, the Vallandigham resolution, calling for an investigation, was tabled at the request of Representative Kellogg of Illinois.[44] Initially, efforts to raise the second-office question also were thwarted during the third session of the Thirty-seventh Congress (1863), when LeGrand Byington claimed the seat held

[43] 42 *Congressional Globe* 2103 (1870).
[44] 31 *Congressional Globe* 3–4th ff., esp. July 4 and 12 (1861).

by William Vandever, a colonel in the volunteers. However, on January 20, 1863, Vandever was declared disqualified for having accepted his commission.

Although the Senate was not faced with the question of one of its member's holding a second office, in a matter involving James Lane of Kansas it indicated that it would unseat anyone who accepted a commission in the volunteers. Lane had been offered a commission, but when he was advised that he would have to resign from the Senate, he refused to accept the appointment. However, the Committee on the Judiciary was convinced that he had accepted a commission and therefore was not entitled to a Senate seat. The committee then proposed that F. P. Stanton be given the oath of office, having been appointed by the governor to fill the apparent vacancy created by Lane's commission and subsequent disqualification. While the senators seemed to be in general agreement that Article I, section 6 was applicable to everyone holding a commission, even though in the state volunteers rather than in the Army of the United States, they decided by a vote of 24 to 16 that Lane was entitled to membership by having turned down the military appointment.[45]

Then, by seating Adelbert Ames in 1870, the Senate in effect reversed itself. Ames said he had resigned his commission in the army after Congress enacted the bill readmitting Mississippi to the Union but before the bill had become law over the President's signature. He also said that the President had accepted his resignation before signing the Mississippi reentry bill. Although these statements were probably true, it is also true that Ames retained his post as provisional governor of Mississippi until after his election to the Senate. In this capacity he had signed his own credentials for election to the Senate by the Mississippi legislature. As was implied in Conkling's statement of March 22, it did not really matter whether the Senate voted against seating Ames. The "carpetbaggers" and "scalawags" were so effectively in control of the political machinery in Mississippi that Ames would be back before the Senate in no time with a new set of credentials.

---

[45] The debate and pertinent data are found in 32 ibid., 115, 128, 263, 393, 340, 360–363 (1862).

Political factors often make it difficult for the House or the Senate to apply standards uniformly and consistently, and this was particularly true after the Civil War. It was also a point upon which Democrats dwelled with some regularity, for they accused the Radicals of using two standards in judging the qualifications of ex-Confederates—one standard for those to whom the test oath of July 1862 was vigorously applied and another for those whose conduct during the war was no less offensive but for whom the test oath was waived. This distinction led the Democrats to charge that the test of loyalty was not to the United States but to the Republican Party. To understand why the Democrats made such charges, we will consider a number of cases that arose between 1867 and 1871.

Application of the Oath of Office Act

At the time of the enactment of the test oath, in July 1862, some congressmen—such as Senators Davis of Kentucky and Saulsbury of Delaware—argued that Congress could not add to the list of constitutional qualifications. The oath clause of Article VI (clause 3) is sufficient authority in itself, Senator Trumbull maintained, an argument also advanced by Sumner during the Stark affair in that same year. The Davis-Saulsbury argument could be refuted, on one hand, by precedents: the permanent disqualification imposed by the Act of 1790 upon those who had bribed federal judges and judges who accepted bribes, and the Act of 1853, which disqualified those who offered bribes to other national officials, officials who accepted bribes, and those who destroyed public documents, records, and papers entrusted to them for safekeeping. On the other hand, these early laws were more than instances in which Congress used its legislative power to prescribe additional disqualifications: a man had to be *convicted* of having committed one of the specified crimes, to incur their permanent disability. But the Test Oath Act of 1862 did not require evidence of such a conviction. It automatically excluded congressmen-elect who could not affirm that they (1) had not borne arms against the United States; (2) had not served in an office under the authority of a government hostile to the United States; and (3) had not given aid, counsel, or countenance to the enemies of the United States. As a disclaimer affidavit, therefore, the Oath of Office Act disqualified all ex-Confederates and Southern sympathizers.

Most likely those who voted for the Oath of Office Bill in 1862 considered it essential to protect future Congresses from being tainted by disloyal persons. However, they discovered that, because of mitigating circumstances or partisan considerations, this disclaimer affidavit should not operate automatically in all instances. It was this anomaly, as well as the arbitrary decisions that often had to be made, that permitted Democrats to accuse Republicans of employing two standards, of condemning some ex-Confederates while forgiving others whose offenses were just as serious.

Both the House and the Senate began to contend with these complex issues in July 1867, when eight of the nine representatives from Kentucky were challenged. Only George M. Adams, who had served in the Union forces, was seated without opposition. The others were challenged either on the ground that they had aided and abetted traitors or that their elections were obtained by ex-rebels and Southern sympathizers who "overawed and prevented from a true expression of their will" the good and loyal people of Kentucky.[46] Several contested elections added to the burden of the Committee on Elections in its efforts to investigate the various kinds of charges and complaints.

In proposing that the credentials of the Kentuckians be referred to committee, Representative Logan asked that the oath of office not be administered until the House had a complete report that was based upon the investigations. Also, his resolution initiated a partisan debate in which Democratic Representative James Brooks of New York introduced a theme that was to be restated as other cases arose: the Republican-dominated House used "loyalty" as meaning loyalty to the Republican Party rather than to the United States. The true purpose of the Republicans, Brooks declared, was to keep Democrats out of Congress. Bitterly partisan comments, offered by each side, did little to focus attention upon the issue of a chamber's constitutional power to judge

---

[46] The debates on seating the Kentucky delegation began July 3, 1867, and continued into the next session, which began Dec. 3, 1867 (38 *Congressional Globe* 468–479, 514, (1867), and 39 ibid., 13, 664, 892–900, 1161 [1867–1868]).

a member-elect. Instead, the situation emphasized the political importance of one party's having so large a majority that it could act arbitrarily in admitting some members-elect and excluding others.

Impacted by various issues, the Kentucky cases warranted the committee's request that it be permitted to take testimony until December 1, 1867. An extension of time was needed, Representative Logan said on July 9, before the committee could answer the "question of the disqualification of these persons holding certificates." By December 3, the committee was able to report favorably on the cases of four members-elect from Kentucky; but in the meantime the Democrats had challenged the seating of various Tennesseans, intending to embarrass the Republicans rather than exclude ex-Confederates.

Representatives Brooks and Eldridge objected to the swearing in of the Tennesseans. At least three of the members-elect, Brooks said, were guilty of treason and of violating the laws and Constitution of the United States. One of the three, R. R. Butler, had been a member of Tennessee's secessionist legislature and therefore was ineligible for the oath prescribed in the Act of July 1862. Moreover—according to Brooks—all of them should be excluded on the ground that at the time of their election Tennessee did not have a republican form of government, as required by the Constitution. Brooks based the last point on the claim that so many whites had been disfranchised by the state's suffrage law that a black oligarchy existed.[47]

Because of their implications for this study, several House and Senate cases must be discussed in greater detail at this point. At the same time, we will compare the circumstances surrounding the several cases and contrast the actions taken by the House and the Senate.

The Kentucky cases were still pending in November 1867, when the Democrats decided to make an issue of admitting the Tennessee delegation. Obviously, the Republican-controlled House would not accept Brooks's charge that Tennessee did not have a republican form of government. But neither could the Republicans disregard the charges made by Brooks, Eldridge, and other Democrats, for this would have lent credence to the

---

[47] Ibid., p. 768 (1867).

claim that the Radicals were misusing God, Scripture, and the Constitution in trodding upon human rights. The Radicals, the Democrats argued, were willing to seat men who had been ardent supporters of the Confederacy and had practiced all the infamy that was daily charged against those who refused to vote with the Republicans. The Democrats said that the Radicals' duplicity was readily apparent: they permitted ex-Confederates to be "marked white by the simple process of an oath taken here"—by falsely denying they were guilty of offenses against the United States.[48]

Although such charges were intended to embarrass the Republican majority, the latter was willing, said Representative Schenck, to accept its responsibilities rather than fall victim to a Democratic ploy. Well might Schenck have been disturbed by Democratic conduct—especially when members on the opposite side of the aisle introduced resolutions to bar certain Tennesseans and then voted against their own proposals. But, aside from their partisan charges and countercharges, these cases from Kentucky, Tennessee, and elsewhere provided meaty issues and ample opportunities for debating the constitutional question, as in the case of William B. Stokes, one of the members-elect from Tennessee, whose loyalty had been questioned.

In a letter of May 10, 1861, to John Duncan, Stokes had written about the illegality of Lincoln's calling up troops to subjugate the South and about the right of revolution.[49] On the other hand, Stokes had served as a colonel in the Union army. When, on July 27, 1866, Representative Eldridge asked Stokes whether he could in good conscience take the oath, Stokes responded that his pro-Union record went back as far as the Compromise Act of 1850. He admitted the error of some of his remarks in his letter to Duncan, but he had not said a single word in favor of secession. Indeed, he had not only worked against Tennessee's secession but, when the Union forces reached Nashville in November 1861, had joined them as a major and was later promoted to colonel. Inasmuch as nothing came of the Duncan letter in July 1866, the Republicans were probably surprised when the Democrats made the letter an issue in November 1867.

---

[48] Ibid., p. 772.

[49] This letter also became an issue earlier in 1866, when Stokes first appeared as a representative from Tennessee. It is found in 36 *Congressional Globe* 4271 (1866).

Although it was important that the Democrats strike as hard as possible at the exceptions the Republicans were permitting to the test-oath statute, the first discussion of the Duncan Letter (in July 1866) had occurred at the very moment the Senate requested that the House pass a joint resolution modifying the Test Oath Act for David T. Patterson. Patterson had been elected a circuit court judge in Tennessee in the 1850s but, according to his testimony, had wanted to resign after his state seceded. However, at the request of the Unionists within the area, he had retained the post. Although his sympathies may not have been with the secessionists, he was technically disqualified from membership in Congress by reason of this provision in the test oath.

I have neither sought nor accepted nor attempted to exercise the functions of any office whatever under any authority, or pretended authority, in hostility to the United States.

Although the Senators believed that mitigating circumstances justified a modification of the test-oath requirement, the House tabled the Senate's resolution. Patterson, however, was given the oath of office on July 28, 1866.[50]

The Duncan letter was but one bit of evidence the Democrats used in 1867 in opposing the Tennesseans; Brooks, for example, also introduced a charge against Representative-elect Mullins. First Lieutenant A. M. Troluger of Tennessee, who had known Mullins since boyhood, reported in a letter of November 12, 1867, that the representative-elect had made disloyal statements near Shelbyville, Tennessee, in 1861. According to Troluger, Mullins had urged young men to join the rebel forces, had said that half of the North and the whole of the South supported the rebellion, had asserted it was "the duty of every Southern man to take side with the South in the struggle."[51] Despite the Democrats' efforts to force the Radicals to accept the precedent they had employed against the Kentucky delegation (conducting inquiries before giving the oath of office to various members), all of the Tennesseans were seated without inquiry except R. R. Butler. It is obvious from their comments that the Democrats did not subscribe to the Kentucky precedent, but they regarded it as a good political ploy to use against the Republicans.

---

[50] Ibid., p. 4293.
[51] 38 *Congressional Globe* 774 (1867).

Nevertheless, the Republicans continued to provide the Democrats with ammunition, as evidenced in the John Young Brown and R. R. Butler cases in the House and the case of Senator-elect Philip F. Thomas of Maryland. Brown was one of the Kentuckians whom the Committee on Elections found was disqualified for having given aid and comfort to those who served in armed rebellion against the United States. Underlying this charge was a letter of April 18, 1861, from Brown to the *Louisville Courier* in which he acknowledged his public utterances against sending a single man or dollar from Kentucky to aid Lincoln in the "unholy war against the South." He had also entreated Kentuckians to resist the Northern armies as they crossed the borders of the state, and he suggested that any man who volunteered for the Union army should be shot down in his tracks.[52] Although there were some in the House who argued that such expressions should be read in the context of the prevailing neutrality sentiment in Kentucky instead of being literally construed, on February 13, 1868, the House voted against seating Brown by reason of his having aided, counseled, and encouraged those in rebellion against the United States.[53]

On February 25, 1868, Representative Dawes, chairman of the Committee on Elections, reported on the charges of disloyalty that had been brought against Butler. Since Butler had been elected to and had served in the secessionist legislature of Tennessee, the question about his loyalty seemed valid. Moreover, because of his service to a Confederate state, Butler could not take the oath of office as prescribed by the Act of July 1862. But the feeling, Dawes declared, was that he had always been a Unionist, and the committee therefore requested that the test oath be waived for Butler, as the Senate had previously done for Patterson. The Democrats argued, however, that the situations in the Brown and Butler cases were not such as to justify the employment of different standards. According to Representative Mungen, ex-Confederates could have eradicated their crimes of assisting and fighting in the war against the Union by voting the Radical ticket.[54]

There was yet another issue in the Butler case—the fact that

[52] Ibid., pp. 664, 892 (1868).
[53] Ibid., p. 1161.
[54] Ibid., pp. 1426, 1662–1665.

his son had joined the Confederate army. But, the younger Butler testified before the committee "My father told me that he would rather see my throat slit from ear to ear than see me in the uniform of the Confederate Army."[55] Should the father bear the political sin of his son? The answer to this question, at least in the Butler and Thomas cases, depended upon the father's actions after the son joined the Confederates.

Although his son's service in the Confederate forces was only one of the issues in the Thomas case, it was the most important factor in the Senate's refusal to seat the senator-elect from Maryland. On March 16, 1867, after his colleague, Reverdy Johnson, presented Thomas's credentials, Senator Howard immediately proposed that the Committee on the Judiciary decide whether Thomas was entitled to membership:

It is matter of common rumor that the gentleman . . . sympathized warmly with the rebels during the late Civil War. One rumor . . . is that he performed an act tending to give aid and comfort to the rebels during the existence of the rebellion.[56]

In fact, several rumors surrounded Thomas. One was that, as Buchanan's Secretary of the Treasury in 1860, he had transferred hundreds of thousands of dollars from New York to New Orleans so that, when war erupted, the rebels could seize these funds. That was not true, Thomas argued; the money had been sent to pay expenses incurred by the national government and all the funds had been disbursed before the outbreak of hostilities. A question also was raised about Thomas's resignation as Secretary of the Treasury because of the Buchanan Administration's decision to strengthen Fort Sumter in South Carolina. This was more than a rumor, for in his letter of resignation Thomas had told the President he disagreed with "constitutional advisers" about the need for strengthening the garrison in South Carolina.[57] Still another matter of consequence was Thomas's alleged statement to a nominating caucus that if he was elected he would go to the Senate "to face those men [the Radical Republicans] who are now and always were traitors to the Union."

---

[55] Ibid., p. 1688.

[56] 38 *Congressional Globe* 171 (1867).

[57] Ibid. This letter was read into the record and was occasionally referred to as evidence of Thomas's disloyalty.

This case increasingly reflected the Senate's division about its power to judge a man on grounds other than those stipulated in the Constitution. Some senators, such as Davis of Kentucky, were willing to give Thomas the oath and then conduct an investigation to determine whether he should be held accountable for slandering the Senate. But there were hardliners on each side of the constitutional issue; and those who favored a complete investigation into the several charges were in a majority. Because of its manifold and complex issues and questions, the Thomas case was to drag on for some time.

On December 18, 1867, the Committee on the Judiciary reported there was insufficient evidence to bar Thomas, "unless it be found in the fact of the son of said Thomas having entered the military service of the confederacy and in the circumstances connected with that fact or relating to it." But the committee made no attempt to judge or evaluate the matter of his son's having entered the Confederate army.[58] In line with the committee's report and findings, Senator Johnson proposed that Thomas be admitted to membership.

Henceforth the debate focused almost exclusively on the Senate's prescribing qualifications in addition to those stipulated in the Constitution and on the issue of Thomas's being ineligible for the oath by reason of his son's joining the Confederate army. Since the House had not used a similar issue to disqualify Butler, there was a question, often propounded, whether Thomas should be treated differently. But some senators distinguished between the cases. When Butler said he would prefer to see his son's throat slit rather than see him in a Confederate uniform, he had demonstrated intense distaste for his offspring's decision. Thomas, on the other hand, though equally opposed to his son's joining the Confederate army, had given him a hundred dollars after failing to persuade him to stay home. "I cannot bear the thought," he had said, "that you are to be a captive in prison and without the means of saving yourself from actual want, without the means, on the contingency of your sickness, of procuring medical aid." To guard against such emergencies, Thomas had given the money to his son.[59]

---

[58] Ibid., p. 243 (1867).
[59] Ibid., p. 322.

How should such an act be judged? Some claimed it was no more than the natural act of a parent concerned about the well-being of his son. Others argued that this was an act of aiding and abetting the enemy, and thus was ample reason for excluding Thomas. The money, Senator Stewart argued, helped young Thomas join the Confederate forces—a conclusion that seemed unjustified since only when the son adamantly declared he was going to enlist had the father given him the money. Thomas had been negligent in meeting his responsibilities as a citizen, declared Senator Sumner, for he had not only aided the enemy by giving the money to his son, but had failed

to disclose and make known the treason of his son to the President or other proper authorities, according to the requirement of the statute in such cases, [and was therefore] guilty of misprision of treason as defined by existing law.[60]

After submitting, considering, and withdrawing several resolutions, the Senate decided to vote on the resolution proposed by Senator Johnson, which declared Thomas eligible for membership and provided for the oath being administered. Immediately after its defeat (by a vote of 28 to 21),[61] Senator Drake offered a resolution that Thomas, "having voluntarily given aid, countenance, and encouragement" to persons engaged in hostile acts against the United States, be declared ineligible to take the oath. This resolution was passed by a vote of 27 to 20, and the governor of Maryland was informed that a Senate vacancy existed.

All of the issues in the Thomas case, even though combined, were no more serious than the charges against many others who had been seated. In resigning as Secretary of the Treasury several months before the commencement of hostilities, he had said nothing more serious than anything said by Stokes and Mullins. And his act of resignation was not more serious than Patterson's retention of his judgeship in Tennessee and Butler's election to Tennessee's secessionist legislature. If Thomas was

---

[60] From Sumner's resolution to exclude Thomas, introduced Feb. 13, 1866 (ibid., p. 1145), but withdrawn in order that another resolution (the one capable of attracting the largest number of votes) could be adopted.

[61] Ibid., p. 1268 (Feb. 19, 1868).

guilty of aiding the enemy by reason of his son's joining the Confederate army, Butler was guilty on the same ground, the statement about throat slitting notwithstanding. And Thomas's alleged slander of the Senate was not more vicious than comments attributed to other members-elect in those years. The Thomas case was but one example of the inconsistent application of standards during the postwar years.

Other Acts of Prior Misconduct

A contested election in Georgia's Sixth Congressional District in 1868 brings to light some of the confusing elements that were common in that day. All but one of the Georgia delegation bore credentials signed by Major General George G. Meade, and the exception, John A. Wimpy, whose credentials were signed by Governor Bullock, challenged the right to membership of one of the former, John Cristy. Wimpy's credentials contained statements acknowledging that Cristy had won a majority of votes within the sixth district but declaring him ineligible by reason of the disability clause in the Fourteenth Amendment. Under Georgia law, the credentials stated, an ineligible victor is to be succeeded by the candidate who has the second highest number of votes.[62]

Representative Brooks spoke of Cristy's devotion to the Union. If Cristy had formally acknowledged the legitimacy of the secessionist government, Brooks claimed, it was only because he had not had the protection of the government of the United States. Indeed, Meade's signature on Cristy's credentials should have refuted any charges about the latter's disloyalty. As the case developed, however, it became apparent that charges of disloyalty could be lodged against both Cristy and Wimpy, and thus the whole matter was turned over to the Committee on Elections.

On January 15, 1868, Chairman Dawes reported that Cristy had indeed aided, counseled, and encouraged the rebels and was not entitled, therefore, to take the oath of office. But the committee also reported against Wimpy. Because he had not won a majority of the votes, Wimpy was not entitled to the seat.[63]

---

[62] 40 *Congressional Globe* 7 (1868).
[63] Ibid., pp. 392–393.

Nothing came of the committee's report, however, for recent developments in Georgia now raised doubts whether the state had a republican form of government. This doubt had a significant impact on the Senate.

When Joshua Hill appeared as a senator-elect from Georgia (also in 1868), objections were made to his being given the oath of office, although no evidence was presented that Hill was either personally or politically disqualified or had been anything but a Unionist during the war.[64] Hill had been elected by an "integrated" Georgia legislature in July 1868, but the following September the white majority in each chamber had expelled all black members.[65] It was because of this action that objections were raised against seating Hill. His credentials, and later those of his colleague, H. V. M. Miller, were referred to the Committee on the Judiciary. On March 17, 1869, the committee reported a bill to enforce the Fourteenth Amendment and the laws of the United States in Georgia, "and to restore to that State the republican form of government elected under its new constitution." Not until action was taken on this bill, the committee recommended, should the Senate consider the credentials of Hill and Miller.[66]

The question about Georgia's being properly reconstructed was but one matter with which the Senate had to contend. In late 1870 and early 1871, it acquired still another problem pertaining to Georgia: credentials from Henry P. Farrow and Richard H.

---

[64] Three years later, when Hill challenged the right of Foster Blodgett to be seated as a senator from Georgia, it became apparent that Hill was as guilty of pro-Confederate activities as Philip Thomas. Senator Stewart of Nevada reported that he had several letters of an incriminatory nature but that he had decided not to use them against Hill. Senator Hill then admitted various statements and actions. Since neither Stewart nor any other senator had made reference to these matters in the chamber, it seems likely that Hill was aware of incriminating letters and their contents. He admitted having written a letter to the governor of Georgia in which he had said that President Davis was ably administering the Confederacy. Hill also said that his sons had served in the Confederate army. While he was visiting a son hospitalized in Richmond, a battle between Union and Confederate forces took place and he had helped administer to the wounded. Hill also referred to a letter (in which he spoke about the value of slavery) whose purpose, Hill claimed, was to subvert a plan proposed by Jefferson Davis to enlist black males and give them freedom in exchange for military service (44 *Congressional Globe* 548–554 [1871]).
[65] 40 *Congressional Globe* 2 (1868).
[66] Ibid., p. 103 (1869).

Whitely, who claimed the two Senate seats, and a certificate of election (presented January 20, 1871) from Foster Blodgett, who claimed the Senate seat whose new six-year term would begin March 4. The Senate was now faced with four Senate claimants who had been elected by different "reconstructed" Georgia legislatures and with a fifth senator-elect whose term of office would begin shortly. After several months of parliamentary maneuvering, Hill was given the oath of office on February 1, 1871, and Miller was seated on February 24. Since Miller's term of office would soon expire, the Senate had to decide whether Foster Blodgett was qualified and should be given the oath of office on March 4.

Blodgett, who had figured prominently in the trial of Andrew Johnson as a witness for the prosecution and a "victim" of the administration's defiance of the Tenure of Office Act, may have been admired by the Radicals. But this predisposition could not remove the stain of a pro-Confederacy past and an indictment for perjury. Senator Hill presented various affidavits, purporting to show why Blodgett was disqualified, that touched upon the number of subjects and charges. Blodgett's election had been obtained from an illegally constituted legislature; he had borne arms against the United States; he had resorted to bribery in winning election; and he had accepted the position of postmaster in his community even though it had been necessary to perjure himself in taking the oath of office. (According to one charge, Blodgett's son had taken the oath of office for his father inasmuch as the latter was unable to make the disclaimers required by the Act of July 1862.) Still other charges were contained in the affidavits presented by Hill. Blodgett had organized vigilantes to murder the Unionists within his community. And an affidavit from J. E. Bryant, dated March 21, 1871, stated that, as superintendent, Blodgett had so maladministered a state-owned railway as to cause Georgia to suffer a financial loss. The affidavit also stated that

it is charged and believed that some of this money was stolen by Blodgett and his friends. It is charged and believed that some of this money was used to bribe members of the Legislature to vote for Blodgett for United States Senator.[67]

---

[67] 44 *Congressional Globe* 542–545 (1871).

We can, of course, view these affidavits in the same light as those presented in the Stark case almost a decade earlier; they were unsubstantiated in some of their allegations and they had been obtained in *ex parte* proceedings. Nevertheless, some of the charges about his previous conduct were sufficiently documented. There could be no doubt, for example, that the United States had tried to prosecute Blodgett for having committed perjury at the time he accepted his postmastership. An indictment had been obtained but the case was dismissed on a technical point; the Government could produce only a certified copy of the oath said to have been rendered by Blodgett. However, the indictment had been the cause for the Postmaster General's removal of Blodgett from office. Since this removal had not been in accord with the procedures stipulated in the Tenure of Office Act of 1867, the Radicals had objected to the dismissal, and President Johnson's defiance of that act (in removing Secretary Stanton) had been one of the other charges in the impeachment proceeding. Thus politics and circumstances had made the ex-Confederate, Foster Blodgett, an ally of the Radicals in their bid to impeach and convict Johnson.[68]

Partisan factors were much in evidence in the Senate's handling of the Blodgett case. There seem to have been ample grounds for summarily excluding him, for enough of the evidence against him was substantiated and fully as serious as the charges that were brought against other congressmen-elect who had been denied the oath of office. However, the Blodgett case was to drag on through the first session of the Forty-second Congress; then, in the following session, Thomas M. Norwood was seated instead of Blodgett. Nevertheless, the Blodgett case presents interesting matters, especially when we consider the battle some of the Radical Republicans made in his behalf and the fact that a Senate committee had recommended that he be given the oath of office.

It was established that Blodgett had held a commission in the Georgia volunteers and thus was automatically excluded by the test oath from serving in any national office, whether as postmaster or senator. The fraudulence surrounding his acceptance of

---

[68] 39 *Congressional Globe* supplement, *The Trial of Andrew Johnson*, pp. 122, 240 (1868).

the postmastership—whether he had sworn to the disclaimer affidavit on his own or had his son take the oath for him—had been made part of the record by the defense in the trial of President Johnson. The indictment that grew out of his accepting this office had been the cause for his removal by the Postmaster General. And although the indictment had been quashed because of a technicality, there was incontrovertible evidence that he had aided and abetted the Confederacy and therefore was disqualified from accepting any national office by provision of the Oath of Office Act of July 1862.

Yet some Radicals treated him with respect and favor, which must have been at least partially motivated by Blodgett's appearance as a witness for the prosecution in the Senate's trial and near conviction of Andrew Johnson. But this hardly justified Blodgett's defense by Senator Stewart of Nevada, who cited him as

the most conspicuous example we have from all of the South of persecution on account of his love for the Union. I think he has been pursued on account of his Union proclivities more severely than any other man.[69]

Though admitting that Blodgett had engaged in acts of rebellion, Stewart claimed that the Georgian had been a loyal Union man before the war. The circumstances surrounding the postmastership had been such that Blodgett felt "he could consider himself loyal, and he took the test-oath."[70]

On April 11, 1871, the Senate voted 19 to 17 to table the resolution to seat Blodgett. The issue now went to the Committee on Privileges and Elections, and the following December it recommended the seating of Norwood. Nothing in its recommendation suggested why the case was being disposed of in this manner. About all we can safely conclude is that, in denying the seat to Blodgett, the Senate did not act because of evidence of disloyalty or deceit but because of the circumstances surrounding Blodgett's election. A case that began with the Senate judging the qualifications of a member-elect became an instance of the Sen-

---

[69] 44 *Congressional Globe* 548 (1871).
[70] Ibid., p. 552.

ate's use of its power to judge the election and returns of one of its members.[71]

"There is joy in Heaven," said Benjamin Butler, "over the one sinner that repenteth." Democratic representatives accepted this as meaning that the sinner who repents is the one who thereupon dons the Republican label. Indeed, said Democratic Representative Wood of New York, the evidence was clear, for in the Thirty-ninth, Fortieth, and Forty-first Congresses the Republican majority had excluded thirty-five Southern Democrats whose crimes had been no more serious than those of ex-Confederate Republicans whom it had seated in the House and the Senate.

At issue in 1870 was the question whether Charles Porter of Virginia should be seated as a representative-elect, and Representative Wood had presented a memorial in objecting to his seating. This memorial, taken from a court-martial record maintained by the War Department, reported certain comments Porter had made in saloons in Norfolk, Virginia, on July 22 and 28, 1864. The government of the United States, Porter said on the first occasion,

is all a G-d d----d humbug from beginning to end, and if you could have seen what I did in Washington you would say so. Abraham Lincoln is doing anything he can for his election. If Abraham Lincoln allows the military authorities to go on as it is here [sic] I would rather live under Jeff. Davis' government than this.[72]

Also included in the memorial was a charge that Porter, who had been discharged from the Union army to become attorney for the Commonwealth of Virginia in Norfolk, had given aid and comfort to the enemies of the United States "by uttering in a loud voice, in the hearing of divers good citizens and some rebel sympathizers . . . seditious, treasonable, and scandalous words." When asked whether he would prefer to live under the Confederacy, Porter had answered: "Yes, by G-d, I stand here and proclaim boldly and above board that the United States Government is a bogus, rotten, and corrupt Government from beginning to end." For such conduct and utterances Charles Porter had been convicted by a military commission and sentenced to confine-

---

[71] 45 ibid., p. 211 (1871).
[72] 42 *Congressional Globe* 823 (1870).

ment for six months. General Benjamin Butler, who had been area commander at that time and was now, in 1870, a member of Congress, "remitted all the onerous portion of the judgment of the commission, because the case and his previous acts showed that Porter had not in fact been disloyal.[73]

Porter had accepted the findings of the military commission "like a good patriot," said Butler. "He did not undertake to get out a writ of *habeas corpus,* as some of my Democratic friends in Indiana did to get out from under punishment." It was on this occasion that Butler invoked Scripture, noting the joy in heaven over the sinner that repents. Although the Democrats were disturbed by the different standards employed by the Radicals, they were not in a position to affect the outcome of any case in which a onetime sinner achieved political salvation. The Democrats proposed that the Porter matter be submitted to committee, but this was no more than a halfhearted gesture inasmuch as they later voted to table their resolution.

Summary

Although the disposition of cases was erratic between 1861 and 1871, there can be little doubt that precedents had been established. The power of each chamber to judge the qualifications of its members had been enlarged by the loyalty issue. Within a relatively short time, indeed even before the end of the Reconstruction era, the broader dimensions of this power were formalized. Still, the constitutional issue continued to plague some members of Congress—just as it did in 1967 when Adam Clayton Powell was denied membership. As cases multiplied and touched on these broader dimensions, however, more and more members of Congress claimed the power to consider qualifications other than age, citizenship, and inhabitancy.

[73] From a telegram Butler sent the *Richmond Enquirer and Examiner* on May 5, 1868, and read into the record in 1870 (42 *Congressional Globe* 823 [1870]).

V

Misconduct, Corruption, and Moral Turpitude: Congressional Scandals of the Late Nineteenth Century

The Civil War, James A. Garfield wrote in 1877, "awakened a reckless spirit of adventure and speculation, and multiplied the opportunities, and increased the temptations to evil."[1] This was hardly an exaggeration. During the war, James F. Simmons of Rhode Island resigned from the Senate rather than face possible expulsion on the charge that he had benefited from the sale of weapons to the armed forces.[2] General William W. Belknap, Grant's Secretary of War, resigned in 1876 rather than risk conviction by the Senate in an impeachment proceeding in which he had been charged with a corrupt practice. Earlier, in 1870, two representatives, B. F. Whittemore of South Carolina and John T. Deweese of North Carolina, resigned after a committee recommended their expulsion for selling appointments to the military academies. And the Credit Mobilier scandals of 1872–73 touched some of the most prominent members of each chamber, including Representative Garfield himself.

---

[1] "A Century of Congress," *Atlantic Monthly* (July 1877), reprinted in 1 *The Works of James Abram Garfield* 487 (1882).

[2] 32 *Congressional Globe* 3061, 3167, 3320 (1862).

There is, then, little wonder that Garfield warned the American people:

If the next centennial does not find us a greater nation, with a great and worthy Congress, it will be because those who represent the enterprise, the culture, and the morality of the nation do not aid in controlling the political forces which are employed to select the men who shall occupy the great places of trust and power.[3]

Well might Garfield have urged the political, business, educational, and moral leaders of the nation to join in this venture of protecting the public trust and power from further abuses. However, such protection demanded more than moral lectures from congressional leaders; it required determination on the part of congressmen to act forcefully and not be, as George F. Hoar declared, "perhaps unconsciously influenced by the desire to shield a political associate from punishment."[4]

In a sense, the issues that arose in the last decades of the nineteenth century were new and unique. Nevertheless, their disposition, as before, depended upon how the chambers viewed their powers to judge and upon which powers they decided to use. Each chamber, of course, could call upon the precedents created during the Civil War and the postwar period. The House and Senate, therefore, were fully able to act resolutely—whenever they chose to act. However, they were also faced with questions to which precedents offered only indefinite answers. How, for example, was either chamber to decide a case in which a congressman who was accused of misconduct, resigned to escape expulsion, was reelected in a special election, and presented new credentials? None of the precedents provided a definitive answer to such a question. Thus, the House and the Senate were in a position to create new precedents if they so desired.

Each house, as before, was also beset by the time factor. There were cases, for example, in which the alleged offenses had been committed before a man's election or reelection. And as was shown in the Credit Mobilier and polygamy cases, offenses could occur either before election or during a previous session of Con-

---

[3] "A Century of Congress" reprint, p. 489.
[4] *Autobiography of Seventy Years* 364–365 (1903). Although Hoar referred to the reluctance of Republican senators to act against General Belknap after he resigned from office, his observation was equally applicable to other situations, especially the Credit Mobilier case.

gress yet be of such a nature that they were also continuing acts of misconduct. These were the kinds of cases that confronted each chamber in the last decades of the nineteenth century.

Corrupt Congressmen

To bring the time factor into better perspective and to note the inexactness of the precedents, this section will discuss the three cases in which representatives were charged with selling appointments to Annapolis and West Point. On February 2, 1870, the *New York Times* ran this pseudo ad:

United States Naval Academy.—Vacant cadetship to be filled before June. Parties of means address 'Congressman,' Box No. 142, Times Office. Also West Point vacancy.

In the estimation of some congressmen, this brief item in the *Times*—together with other items and news reports—might do great harm both to the academies and to Congress. It was therefore proposed that the matter be investigated by the Committee on Military Affairs,[5] and between February 21 and March 16, 1870, this committee reported adversely on three representatives: B. F. Whittemore of South Carolina, J. T. Deweese of North Carolina, and R. R. Butler of Tennessee.

The first of these committee reports implicated Whittemore; he had, the committee disclosed, "been influenced by improper pecuniary considerations" in making appointments to the academies. The committee then recommended that he be expelled from the House.[6] Similar findings and recommendations were made in the Deweese and Butler cases. There was evidence, the committee reported, that Butler accepted $900 "with the avowed intention of using the same for political purposes in the State of Tennessee." The money had been obtained from General Tyler to procure an appointment to West Point for Tyler's son, who, the committee said, was not even a resident of Butler's congressional district. The outcomes of these cases were quite different.

Since the committee had initially reported against Whittemore, this became the test case, and significant issues and ques-

---

[5] 42 *Congressional Globe* 1041 (1870).

[6] The committee's report and recommendation are found in ibid., pp. 1469–1472.

tions were propounded during the debate on a resolution to expel him. For one thing, several members contended that the sale of cadetships had become so widespread that it was sanctioned by custom. Other representatives raised procedural questions when some of their colleagues insisted that this was the kind of situation that was covered by existing legislation. It was true, of course, that by an act of 1853 persons convicted of offering bribes to public officials and public officials convicted of accepting bribes were permanently disqualified for national office. However, a committee's findings of wrongdoing could scarcely be a conviction in the statutory sense.

Whittemore was not expelled; instead, on February 23, 1870, he submitted a letter of resignation. The same course was followed by Deweese, who resigned the day before the committee reported against him. Thus, both men escaped the shame of being expelled; yet each was thereafter censured.[7] Butler, on the other hand, retained his seat in the House and was no more severely punished. A sizable vote in favor of Butler's expulsion fell short of the necessary two-thirds, but a resolution to censure him was adopted 158 to 0.[8]

Butler led a charmed political life. Just a few years before this censure, the test oath had been waived so that he, a one-time member of the secessionist Tennessee legislature, could be admitted to Congress. Then in 1870 he had taken a chance that neither Whittemore nor Deweese dared take. He successfully withstood the expulsion move and suffered no greater penalty than the two men who had resigned.

Butler's continued presence in the House, and the fact that his offense was as serious as Whittemore's, could have justified leniency in the latter's second case. After resigning, Whittemore had been returned to the House in a special election; however, the house disregarded this popular expression of approval. In July, it obtained by exclusion what in February it had hoped to obtain by expulsion.

---

[7] Ibid., pp. 1547, 1616.

[8] Ibid., p. 2002. Although the biographies and autobiographies of several prominent congressmen and public officials of the nineteenth century (James A. Garfield, James G. Blaine, Shelby Cullom, George F. Hoar, and S. S. Cox) refer to the scandals of those years, none discusses the Butler, Deweese, and Whittemore cases. In fact, they make no reference whatsoever to any of these men.

On July 18, 1870, after Whittemore had presented his new credentials, a skirmish over administering him the oath of office was initiated by Representatives Logan and Farnsworth. Logan argued that all the evidence was in, the committee's report of the previous February established Whittemore's guilt, and therefore his credentials should not be accepted. Farnsworth proposed a new committee investigation to determine the relevancy of precedents and to provide guidelines to the House in exercising its power in this instance.

Three days after Whittemore's reappearance, Logan proposed that he be excluded, and again invoked the provision that permanently disqualifies persons convicted of offering and accepting bribes. Since Whittemore had not been convicted in a court of law, Logan was asked how the statute could be applied to the case at hand. He answered:

Sir, I hold the doctrine to be well settled that any legislative or deliberative body, such as this, in considering offenses of this kind, in violation of its rules or the laws of the land, acts judicially and has the power to do that which it may deem necessary to protect itself in the premises.[9]

There can be little doubt that the House and the Senate acts as a tribunal in judging its members. But whether adverse findings by a congressional committee are tantamount to a conviction within the usual statutory definition is open to doubt. Logan, in fact, was trying to justify a claim for broad authority in either chamber to judge the conduct of its members. In effect, then, he was resorting to the same kinds of arguments that had been raised many years earlier in the case of Senator John Smith. Both Buckner Thruston and John Quincy Adams had on that occasion asserted a judicial power for the Senate, and one that the chamber could exercise without reference to constitutional safeguards or rules of evidence.[10]

In requesting that the House exclude Whittemore because he had "disqualified himself from being a member of this body," Logan introduced the constitutional issue into the debate. Admittedly, he said, the House may not deny membership to a man because of his politics or religion. However, it has "the right to

---

[9] Ibid., p. 4670.
[10] See chap. 1 above, pp. 9 and 10.

say that he shall not be a man of infamous character." Unless the House were permitted to exclude such a person, he said, a single congressional district could destroy the nation by electing a representative who would sell his vote.[11] Such a doctrine, Eldridge retorted, undermined the basic principle of representative government. Logan answered that the people do not have the right to "destroy their own liberties by filling Congress with men who, from their conduct, show themselves capable of the destruction of the Government."

The subsequent discussion, in which the members tried to determine the relevance of such precedents as the Brooks, Keitt, and Matteson cases, at least pointed out an apposite feature. When, on earlier occasions, Representatives Giddings, Brooks, and Keitt (among others) returned to the same session of Congress with a new popular mandate, the House had accepted the judgment of the people rather than sought vindication for its own prior action. This, declared Farnsworth, should be the governing principle in the Whittemore case as well.[12] By adopting Logan's resolution, Farnsworth warned, the House could be setting a dangerous precedent that might have irreversible consequences.

By voting 130 to 24 (with 76 abstentions) to exclude Whittemore, the House acted in the same manner as the House and the Senate had acted on earlier occasions when ex-Confederates and rebel sympathizers had been refused membership. The Whittemore decision, now available as a precedent, also served to solidify the arguments that had been advanced by such ideologically different senators as Butler of South Carolina, Davis of Mississippi, and Sumner of Massachusetts. Whether, as Farnsworth declared, the Whittemore case created a dangerous precedent was still to be seen. But shortly thereafter, when the House turned its attention to the Credit Mobilier cases, it acted as though it had never heard of B. F. Whittemore. Its disposition of the Oakes Ames and James Brooks cases in 1873 revealed not only an inherent inconsistency between what the House said it could do and what it did but an inconsistent application of standards of its own making.

---

[11] 42 *Congressional Globe* 4670 (1870).

[12] See his analyses of these cases and his discussion about the right of the people to choose their own representative in ibid., p. 4673.

Between 1872 and 1893, charges of misconduct against members of the House and Senate usually originated during an election campaign or in newspaper accounts, and the accused inevitably requested an investigation so as to clear themselves of the charges. Since, however, so many of these charges were regarded as mere rumors or campaign tactics, the requests for investigation were denied.[13] But other incidents, growing out of the Credit Mobilier affair and a scandal that involved mail subsidies, compelled the attention of the House and Senate. Now, equipped with a number of relevant precedents, notably the Whittemore decision, the House could have been expected to act in accord with them in the Credit Mobilier case. That the House chose not to use its full arsenal of resources can be attributed to the fact that prominent members of each party were implicated.

On December 2, 1872, an investigation was urged on the basis of reports that Representative Oakes Ames of Massachusetts had bribed other members "to perform certain legislative acts for the benefit of the Union Pacific Railway Company by presents of stock in the Credit Mobilier of America [a corporation which built the rail lines in the West under a subsidy from the United States], or by presents of a valuable character derived therefrom."[14] There was no need for action by the House, Representative Archer declared, since the issue had already been heard by a higher tribunal, the voters, and they had reelected Ames.

In analyzing this case, we should bear in mind the disposition of the Matteson and Whittemore cases. Ames's case was similar to Matteson's in that the former's alleged offense also occurred during a previous Congress. Presumably, therefore, given the Matteson decision, the jurisdiction of the House had ended with the adjournment of that Congress. On the other hand, Ames's offense could be said to be a continuing offense because of his constant purpose to effect legislation favorable to the Union Pacific. In that sense, then, the House could judge his conduct just as it had judged Whittemore's.

---

[13] Examples are the reported charges against W. J. Purman (4 *Congressional Record* 1560 [1876]), Charles Hays (ibid., p. 1604), James G. Blaine (ibid., p. 2724), Oliver P. Morton (ibid., p. 2900), and Thomas C. Power (25 ibid. 46 [1893]). On each occasion requests for investigation were denied.

[14] From the preamble to the Blaine resolution for a committee investigation (46 *Congressional Globe* 11 [1872]).

Despite many objections, charges against Ames were investigated. According to the committee's report of February 13, 1873, Ames had contracted with the Union Pacific in 1867 to build 667 miles of railroad at a total cost of $47 million, which was to be shared by the stockholders of Credit Mobilier, who were also large stockholders in the Union Pacific. Because of this contract, the value of Credit Mobilier stock increased, but Ames had permitted various members of Congress to purchase shares in Credit Mobilier at par value, even though the stock was doubling in value at that moment, and would soon quadruple. There could be no conflict of interest, Ames reportedly told his fellow congressmen in offering them the opportunity to purchase the stock, since the Union Pacific already had all the land grants and legislation it needed.

But the committee concluded that there was another important factor. Although the Union Pacific had all the land grants and legislation it desired, Ames was looking for "friends in Congress who would resist any encroachment upon or interference with the rights and privileges already secured, and to that end wishes to create in them an interest identical with his own."[15] As an example of legislative issues of importance to the railroad, the committee cited proposals by Midwestern congressmen that the Union Pacific's rates be regulated. Indeed, the committee reported, such proposals were pending at the time Ames approached his colleagues with his offer of shares of Credit Mobilier at par value.

Although several members of the House and Senate were identified as owners of Credit Mobilier stock,[16] only two, Oakes Ames and James Brooks, were charged with misconduct. The charge against Ames was that he had tried to influence legislation through his stock offers. Brooks, as a member of Congress and one of the government's directors of the Union Pacific (a second office which apparently was acceptable in the meaning of Article

---

[15] The committee report appears in ibid., pp. 1462–1466.

[16] Representative Hoar identified three senators and fifteen representatives in addition to Ames. Their prominence, and therefore their importance to Ames and the Union Pacific, can be seen in the fact that two became Vice President, one (Garfield) became President, two later served as Speaker of the House, five were candidates for the presidency, several were or later became chairmen of important legislative committees, and nine representatives were later elected to the Senate. (1 *Autobiography of Seventy Years* 318).

I, section 6), was charged with a conflict of interest. He had obtained fifty shares of stock in the name of his son-in-law, but he was the true owner and beneficiary. These actions of Ames and Brooks were seen as violations of the antibribery legislation, and the committee recommended that both men be expelled.

If Ames's offense was considered the single offense of making stock available to colleagues at less than its market value, the Matteson decision would seem to have been applicable and the House could not have claimed jurisdiction. On the other hand, if it was decided that his purpose was to build and maintain influence for the Union Pacific among members of Congress, his offense was a repeated, continuing, and present occurrence. As long as farmers were organizing to obtain rate-setting legislation, as was constantly evidenced at both the state and the national levels, every congressman who owned shares in Credit Mobilier and was called upon to vote for or against such legislation was indeed involved in a pecuniary interest identical to Ames's. Similarly, by reason of his official positions and as a stockholder, Brooks was guilty of a conflict of interest. The question for the House was whether the offenses were committed during a previous Congress and thus beyond its jurisdiction, or whether the Ames and Brooks actions were such as to bring their cases within the House's jurisdiction in 1873.

By recommending expulsion for each man, the committee took the side of those who argued that each chamber can exercise broad authority. Arrayed against such claims were the arguments of Representatives Beck and Butler. The Credit Mobilier transaction had been completed during a previous Congress, Beck declared; therefore the House had no authority to judge the cases. He would rely, he said, on the courts and the constituencies to right whatever wrongs had been committed.[17] In a similar vein, Representative Butler charged that the committee wanted to judge a man "for an offense committed more than three years before his election [to the current Congress], of which he stands unconvicted by the verdict of any jury or the judgment of any court."[18]

Butler's remarks merit special notice because they contradict

---

[17] Ibid., p. 1817.
[18] Ibid., appendix, p. 176.

what he said three years earlier as a leading advocate for excluding John C. Conner of Texas. Before his election to Congress, a military tribunal had ruled there was insufficient evidence to charges that Conner, an army officer, had mistreated Negro soldiers under his command and then bribed several of them not to testify against him. Of the Conner case, which arose at the same time as the Whittemore case, Butler said:

Now, we have been turning out a man for being bribed to appoint a cadet, and I think we should be careful about letting in a man who will bribe witnesses to commit perjury.[19]

Butler had argued that Conner be excluded, even though the alleged offenses had occurred before his election to Congress and the military tribunal had not found him guilty. In the Ames case, nevertheless, Butler argued for a sharp curtailment of the judicial power of the House. Now there had to have been a conviction in a court of law; now the House could *not* take jurisdiction over an act of misconduct that preceded the election of an accused congressman. Thus, Butler's arguments in the Conner and the Ames cases were wholly inconsistent. And the House was no less inconsistent in disposing of both the Ames and the Brooks cases, not only because it defied clearly apposite precedents but because it imposed a mild form of punishment while claiming it had no jursidiction over the cases.

Resolutions were introduced over a period of several days that approached the issues in a different manner. One, proposed by Representative Sargent, noted that the alleged offenses took place five years earlier and that "grave doubts exist as to the rightful exercise by this House of its power to expel a member" for offenses committed during a previous Congress.[20] Representative Ritchie's resolution stated that, although there was insufficient evidence of wrongdoing by the members named in the committee report (Ames, Brooks, Garfield, Dawes, Scofield, Bingham, and Kelley), the transactions "were corrupting in tendency, pernicious in example, and grossly improper in members of Congress"; therefore, all seven men deserved severe censure and rebuke.[21]

On February 27 Sargent modified his original resolution. Its

---

[19] 42 *Congressional Globe* 2323 (1870).
[20] 46 ibid., 1825 (1873).
[21] Ibid., p. 1826.

preamble still expressed grave doubt whether the House had the power of expulsion for misdeeds committed before the reelection of a member, but it included the proposal that the House "absolutely" condemn the conduct of Ames and Brooks. And the House, by substantial margins, "absolutely" censured Ames (182 to 36) and Brooks (174 to 32).[22] Thus it perpetrated a basic fallacy and inconsistency between assertion and action.

Inasmuch as the House asserted grave doubt whether it had the power to expel a member for an offense committed five years earlier, how could it justify its action in censuring a member for the same offense? Article I, section 5(2) of the Constitution provides:

Each house may determine the rules of its proceedings, punish its members for disorderly behaviour, and, with the concurrence of two thirds, expel a member.

Since the power to censure and the power to expel claim the same constitutional basis, and since the power to punish, whether by censure or expulsion, is applicable only to its members, the House could not logically doubt or deny that it had one power but not the other. This act of censure, therefore, was an expedient device for protecting two esteemed colleagues while making a concession to the public trust. According to the reporter, Butler's characterization of Ames as "an honest man, a patriotic man, a truthful man, and we are to expel him lest we should be contaminated [by his] honesty, truth, and patriotism," was met by applause.[23]

At least one member of the Senate was openly named in these scandals. On February 4, 1873, Vice President Schuyler Colfax, the Senate's presiding officer, read a message from the House revealing that its Credit Mobilier investigations disclosed a matter of importance to the Senate. Proceeding with its own inquiry, the Senate created a select committee, which on February 27—within a week of the conclusion of that session of Congress and James W. Patterson's term in the Senate—recommended that

---

[22] Ibid., pp. 1830–1831. Several years later Representative Hoar reported that Brooks died before the vote was taken and that "Ames felt the disgrace very keenly, and did not live very long afterward" (1 *Autobiography of Seventy Years* 324 [1903]).

[23] Ibid., appendix, p. 178.

Patterson (of New Hampshire) be expelled. Although he had not been reelected, Patterson, hoping to clear his name, requested that action be taken on the committee's recommendation, but his proposal came on March 3, the last day of the session. Because of other pressing matters, the Senate let Patterson's request lie over until it went into executive session, and the matter dragged on during a special session that lasted through the remainder of the month, when Patterson was no longer a member. A resolution of March 14 stated that there had been no time to act in the Patterson case and, since it was questionable whether the Senate could expel someone who was no longer a member, the failure to act should not be interpreted as registering either approval or disapproval of Patterson's conduct.[24]

Although in some respects the facts in the Pacific mail subsidy case were similar to those in the Credit Mobilier scandal, the disposition of the former was quite different. During the Forty-third Congress the Ways and Means Committee had investigated allegations of corruption in procuring the passage of the China-service mail subsidy bill. Then on January 24, 1876, during the first session of the Forty-fourth Congress, Representative Morrison proposed that the investigation be taken up by the Committee on the Judiciary. Its report was not made until the following August, when both the committee's majority and minority announced that two members of the House, William S. King and John G. Schumaker, had received large sums of money to influence passage of the mail subsidy bill in the Forty-third Congress. At that time Schumaker was a member of the House, but King was the House postmaster.[25]

The difference of opinion within the Judiciary committee was caused by the fact that during the Forty-third Congress, the House had adopted a resolution whereby all the relevant docu-

---

[24] 1 *Congressional Record* 195–197 (1873). Although Senators Henry Wilson of Massachusetts and James A. Bayard of Delaware were also implicated, they were exonerated (Hoar, 1 *Autobiography of Seventy Years* 317–319). Vice President Colfax was also implicated, but the Senate's attention was diverted from his possible involvement as a stockholder to a case in which it was alleged that he had "received large sums of money from a person for whom he had obtained a lucrative Government contract." His term expired before any action was taken, and he died shortly thereafter. Ibid., p. 319.

[25] King was elected to the Forty-fourth Congress as a representative from Minnesota.

ments, testimony, and data collected by the Committee on Ways and Means had been turned over to the United States district attorney. Since judicial action on the subsidy case was pending, a majority of the Judiciary Committee decided that the matter was no longer within the jurisdiction of the House. It was also argued that the Humphrey Marshall case (1796) had established the precedent that certain constitutional safeguards had to be available to the accused (though they had been all but ignored in the intervening years) and that the House could not take jurisdiction if the offenses were committed during a previous Congress and /or prior to the election. Four representatives—Lord, Lawrence, Hoar, and Caulfield—nevertheless claimed that the House had jurisidiction. They also proposed that another investigation be made by the Committee on Civil Service Reform "to ascertain and report the facts."

Nothing came of the investigations; nor were there any formal votes on recommendations or proposals. Members of the House were content that the case was properly before the courts; therefore they did not have to act. King and Schumaker are listed as having attended the next session of the Forty-fourth Congress, but there is no indication that they took an active part in it.[26] Neither man was a candidate for reelection to the Forty-fifth Congress.

Other more or less notorious cases of misconduct involved a near-brawl between Representatives Weaver and Sparks and an attempt to censure Representative Van Voorhis of New York. Weaver and Sparks almost came to blows when, in a heated debate, they called each other a liar. The House immediately adjourned and the two men were forcibly kept apart. The next day, December 22, 1880, after several members raised the question of suitable punishment, it was recommended that apologies be required, as had been the practice before the Civil War. Another representative proposed that the two men be expelled. A third proposal was that a select committee be appointed to inquire into the situation and make a recommendation. However, the entire matter was tabled and no further action was taken.[27]

The Van Voorhis incident arose from comments this represent-

---

[26] The index of the 5 *Congressional Record* (1876–1877) does not list any bills, resolutions, remarks, or votes for either man.
[27] 11 ibid., 311, 329–331 (1880).

ative made while speaking against a rider to the appropriations bill, a provision that pertained to the Sacramento River in California:

Nobody would have heard of such a thing as that if the Chairman of the Committee on Commerce were not from California. It is outrageous, so damnable, that nobody but a gambler or a cut-throat would have thought of tacking such a thing as that to such a bill as this.[28]

There was an immediate reaction to the language Van Voorhis had used, and some representatives said that even a heated debate did not justify the use of vituperative language toward another member. After an unsuccessful motion to expel Van Voorhis, a resolution to censure him was put to a voice vote, and the speaker announced that the ayes had it. However, after a request for a division and calling of the roll, the resolution was defeated 78 to 66.[29] Then, after it was proposed that he express his regret for using intemperate language, Van Voorhis apologized.

The Weaver-Sparks and Van Voorhis affairs ended so quickly that they barely made the pages of the *Congressional Record*. Not so the Cannon case, which began December 2, 1873, and was not resolved until April 19, 1882.

George Q. Cannon was the first of three Mormons to face the possibility of exclusion or expulsion because of polygamy and/or religious beliefs. How strongly some Americans felt not only about polygamy but what they regarded as a violation of the principle of separation of church and state was shown in President Garfield's inaugural address on March 4, 1881.

The Territories of the United States are subject to the direct legislative authority of Congress; and hence the general government is responsible for the violation of the Constitution in any of them. It is therefore a reproach to the government, that, in the most populous of the Territories, the constitutional guarantee is not enjoyed by the people, and the authority of Congress is set at naught. The Mormon Church not only offends the moral sense of mankind by sanctioning polygamy, but prevents the administration of justice through the ordinary instrumentalities of law.[30]

---

[28] 14 ibid., 3540 (Mar. 1, 1883).
[29] Ibid., p. 3542.
[30] 2 *The Works of James Abram Garfield* 794 (1882).

It is unlikely that Garfield came to such strong views only at the moment of his ascendancy to the highest office of the land. And yet in the preceding nine years, while he was a representative, he and his colleagues had consented to sit in the House with Cannon, the delegate from the Territory of Utah, who was a Mormon and a polygamist.

At the time Cannon first presented himself to the House a resolution had been introduced proposing that, since he had taken oaths "inconsistent with citizenship of the United States and with his obligations as Delegate in this House," and since he "has been, and continues to be, guilty of practices in violation and defiance of the laws of the United States," Cannon's credentials should be submitted to the Committee on Elections and he should not be seated until its report was in.[31] This motion was tabled, and Cannon was given the oath of office on December 2, 1872, but later in that session the polygamy issue was directly raised after Cannon's election was contested. George Maxwell claimed the seat, arguing that fraudulence had been committed in the election.

The Committee on Elections which investigated this charge found that some fraudulent votes had been cast but that throwing them out would not affect Cannon's 18,000 vote plurality.[32] But although it admitted that Cannon had been "elected and returned" as the delegate from Utah, the committee did not say that he was therefore entitled to membership in the House. Testimony had been taken that Cannon had four wives, and he was charged with violation of the antipolygamy act of July 1, 1862. After extensive debate, the House adopted a resolution declaring Cannon "entitled" to serve as the delegate from Utah. It also voted for a resolution that the Committee on Elections investigate the charges about polygamy and that the House be advised of what action it could appropriately take.[33]

Two points are relevant to our analysis of the Cannon case. First, in 1824 there had been objections to the seating of Delegate Gabriel Richard of the Territory of Michigan, who had been a citizen of the United States for only one year prior to his election. On that occasion the House had ruled that the office of delegate, created by the Continental Congress, was not mentioned

[31] 2 *Congressional Record* 7 (1873).
[32] The committee reported its findings May 12, 1874 (ibid., p. 3813).
[33] Ibid., p. 3819.

by the Constitution, and that territorial delegates did not have to meet the same requirements as representatives. Whether this ruling could be enlarged to include extra-constitutional qualifications for delegates might have been an appropriate topic for inquiry by the Elections Committee, but there is no indication that the House was aware of the Michigan precedent. The feeling of members in 1873 and 1874 seemed to be that, in being judged for eligibility, delegates are on an equal footing with representatives.

Second, polygamy is a unique kind of offense in that, unlike most other violations of law, it is continuous. Thus, the time factor, which had been critical in the Matteson, Ames, and Brooks cases, was confused—or perhaps clarified—by the fact that Cannon could be charged with breaking the law of 1862 the moment he had become a polygamist. But his act of entering into marriage with his fourth wife in 1865 (apparently his only marriage after the passage of the antipolygamy statute of 1862) meant that he had committed an offense long before his election as a delegate; therefore, the time factor as it had been applied in the Matteson, Ames, and Brooks cases would seem to be applicable. However, because polygamy is a continuous state, it was not just Cannon's *entering* into multiple marriages that constituted an offense for which he could have been indicted; the act of *living* in polygamy also was a violation of the law.

Thus it would seem that he was guilty of an ongoing offense as well as an offense committed prior to his election. Under these circumstances, the House might have claimed continuing jurisdiction; however, there were those who contended that Cannon's offense was not self-evident; unless he were indicted and convicted in a court of law, there were no grounds on which the House could act either to exclude or to expel him.[34]

---

[34] In his state-of-the-Union message in 1875, President Grant said that new antipolygamy legislation was needed because the 1862 act was so difficult to enforce. It is also noteworthy, however, that at no time in the decade Cannon spent in the District of Columbia did the government make any effort to have him indicted and prosecuted, even though a legislative committee had declared him to be a polygamist and therefore in violation of the laws of the United States. Lenience in this matter might well have been dictated by the social problems that would have been created had the United States acted vigorously under the antipolygamy statute of 1862. This problem was defined by Brigham Young in 1869, when he told visitors from the East: "You would have us put away

Not until February 9, 1875, did the House take up the committee report. The majority report said that Cannon was not worthy to be in the House by reason of his defiance of the law, and recommended "that he be excluded therefrom." Evidence had been submitted, the majority stated, "and not controverted by said Cannon," that he was a polygamist. Having married his fourth wife in August 1865, he was "in open and notorious violation" of the antipolygamy statute. The Committee's recommendation to exclude Cannon was tabled as the House voted not to consider the resolution at that time.[35]

Inasmuch as this decision was taken near the end of that session of Congress, it is quite possible that the House members felt the pressure of more important work, or hoped that Cannon would not be reelected. But Cannon was reelected regularly thereafter, and appeared at the beginning of each Congress with a new set of credentials. Moreover, his polygamous state did not seem to bother the members of the House, who took no further action on the matter until they were forced to do so by public opinion.

Groups from all over the United States began to petition the House, requesting that Cannon be unseated. Petitions were received in each session and duly included in the *Record;* even women in Utah submitted such a petition. On January 12, 1880, it was announced that the Women's Anti-Polygamy Society of the Territory of Utah had requested Cannon's expulsion because of alleged violations of the law relating to polygamy, and this petition was submitted to the Committee on the Judiciary. Although no committee report or recommendation was made during the second session of the Forty-sixth Congress,[36] the petitions had a cumulative effect. When a second Utah election was contested after the elections of 1880, the House was disposed to act more vigorously than it had in the past, even though the arguments of the claimant, Allen G. Campbell, had little validity.

Although Cannon had obtained more than 18,000 votes against Campbell's 1,000 plus, the latter challenged Cannon in a letter to

---

our wives, with whom we are living in lawful wedlock according to the tenets of our church. To do so would be a cruel wrong to our women . . . and their children,—what would become of them?" (Clark E. Carr, *My Day and Generation,* p. 32 [1908]).

[35] 3 *Congressional Record* 1083 (1875).

[36] 10 *Congressional Record* 292 (1880).

the governor of the territory, arguing that Cannon was an "unnaturalized alien" who lived openly with four wives and advocated polygamy. Thus Cannon, Campbell contended, also was inciting others to violate the law. Even if he were to be naturalized, Campbell said, Cannon could not qualify as a delegate, since he was not of good moral character. Campbell also claimed fraudulence in that women had been enfranchised and had so outnumbered males that they delivered the election to Cannon.

Although Cannon was born in England and had come to the United States as a minor, the court of the Territory of Utah provided evidence that Cannon was naturalized before his eighteenth birthday. However, the Territory's supreme court voided the naturalization papers because they had never been recorded. And when the governor issued Cannon the certificate of election, Campbell introduced his objections to the House.[37]

The contested election, the citizenship issue, and other charges forced the House to take another look at Cannon's qualifications.

On January 10, 1882, citing the facts that Cannon admitted being a polygamist and speaking in behalf of this tenet of the Mormon Church, Representative Haskell introduced a resolution that "as the fixed and final determination of the House of Representatives of the Forty-Seventh Congress . . . no person guilty of living in polygamous marital relations, or guilty of teaching or inciting others so to do, is entitled to be admitted to this House . . . as a Delegate from any Territory of the United States."[38] It became the primary responsibility of a House committee to investigate the election and make recommendations. On February 28, 1882, the committee reported that neither Cannon nor Campbell was qualified to be the delegate from the Utah territory.[39] But it was not until April 18 that the House turned its attention to the committee's report and recommendation.

The committee had dismissed the noncitizenship charge, finding that Cannon was in fact a citizen of the United States. The committee also noted that under the terms of the new antipolygamy statute, the Edmunds Act, no polygamist in areas under the exclusive control of the United States could stand for public office or exercise the voting privilege. Nor could he be appointed

[37] 13 *Congressional Record* 35–39 (1881).
[38] Ibid., p. 339.
[39] 40 ibid., 1492.

to any office of trust or profit under the United States.[40] Neverthe-less, many members were still concerned about the procedural question. No matter what evidence a congressional committee might compile to prove that Cannon was a polygamist, the fact remained that he had not been convicted of violating either of the antipolygamy statutes. A resolution declaring that Cannon had been duly elected was defeated. Seventy-nine representatives voted for it, 123 voted against it, and 89 did not vote.[41]

Misconduct before Election

Although some of the foregoing cases involved questions of misconduct during a representative's previous term as a member of Congress, the disposition of these cases varied from each other, as was true of cases that arose from the Civil War. Because hard and fast rules were not developed, the House and the Senate had a large number of precedents from which they could choose. This circumstance not only fortified congressional claims of a discretionary authority but further illustrates the inconsistencies in the exercise of congressional power, because neither the House nor the Senate seemed inclined to set standards or guidelines.

The first case in the late nineteenth century in which a consti-tutional issue was at core involved a Democratic representative who presented his credentials in 1870, after Texas resumed its full role of statehood. In some respects, John C. Conner's offenses were in the same class as others—for example, those of Charles Porter. Conner had made disparaging remarks about the United States government in general and Congress and the military government in Texas in particular, but the most critical charge against him grew out of his mistreatment of black troops under his command, for which he was tried before a military tribunal. A captain in the United States Army, Conner "discovered that the only argument they [the Negro soldiers] would comprehend was the lash." It was used freely, he said, "in the good old Democratic style."[42]

---

[40] See Hazleton's discussion about the pertinency of the Edmunds Act to Cannon's case in ibid., p. 3001.

[41] Ibid., p. 3074 (1882).

[42] From an affidavit alleging that these and similar comments were made at Boston, Texas, on Oct. 20, 1869 (42 *Congressional Globe* 2322 [1870]).

These statements were contained in affidavits presented by Representative Shanks, who objected to Conner's seating and based his argument largely on the fact that Conner had been tried for administering cruel punishment to black soldiers—the military court had ruled there was insufficient evidence to establish guilt. But this decision, the anti-Conner forces contended, had been reached because—as the member-elect admitted—he had bribed the Negro witnesses for the prosecution.

Three forms of objections to the effort to deny Conner membership were raised during the debates. Brooks of New York injected the constitutional issue, declaring that the House did not have the power to judge Conner on any other grounds. Representative Van Trump objected on procedural grounds: Shanks' affidavits had been obtained in *ex parte* proceedings in which Conner had not had the opportunity to confront his accusers and to controvert their allegations. Representative Stevenson objected on the ground that this was another case in which the Republican majority discriminated against Democratic members-elect.

We might recall at this point that Benjamin Butler had supported the seating of Porter of Virginia, a Unionist who had made derogatory statements about the government of the United States, for which he had been tried and found guilty by a military commission. Representative Butler also objected, three years later, to the attempt to oust Oakes Ames, contending that the latter had not been convicted in a court of law. In the interim, however, Butler followed a different tack in the Conner case. The House, he declared, may inquire into anything that pertains to a member-elect. For example, it could raise questions about the statements attributed to Conner in which he had implied that he was "guilty of subornation of perjury in order to clear himself from the charge of cruelty" to the blacks under his command.[43]

Although Conner was given the oath of office, this case transcended the question of the competency of a chamber to judge the pre-election conduct of a member; there were also the allegations of *ex parte* proceedings and the claim that the effort to exclude Conner was motivated by partisanship. With respect to the last

---

[43] Ibid., p. 2325.

point, it should be noted that the Republicans held almost three-fourths of the seats in the House and could have excluded Conner with minimum difficulty in a party-line vote.

Within a period of only a few years in the 1870s, the Senate heard several charges that some of its members had obtained their election by fraudulent means. On March 5, 1872, Senator Caldwell of Kansas made reference to such allegations about himself and his fellow Kansan, Pomeroy, when he announced that the Kansas legislature was investigating charges of bribery and corruption in the 1867 and 1871 elections. Because the only documentation in the Senate's hands was a *Leavenworth Daily Times* report of a joint legislative committee, some senators objected to a Senate investigation. According to Pomeroy, only one chamber of the state legislature was willing to submit relevant materials. Thus, although he was a victim of charges and rumors of bribery, the Senate could not conduct an inquiry in the absence of more substantial documentation.[44]

Indeed, the Senate had voted to table a resolution to investigate the matter, but later it initiated a committee investigation. Inasmuch as Pomeroy had been elected in 1867 and his term was near its end, the committee took up this case first, and concluded that his election by a substantial majority of the state legislators (84 to 25) disproved the charges against him. There was no evidence of wrongdoing, the committee reported. Nevertheless, because of the persistence of the charges, a select committee was created in February 1873 to conduct another investigation of Pomeroy, and its report was submitted March 3, the last day of Pomeroy's six-year term. The majority of this committee also concluded that there was no substantial evidence of bribery.

The Committee on Privileges and Elections, which reported on the Caldwell matter during a special session in 1873, claimed that Caldwell had not been duly elected to the Senate. However, Caldwell argued that

bribery of members of the [state] legislature to vote for a candidate is not made a criminal offense by any statute of the United States,

---

[44] Material about the Pomeroy and Caldwell cases is found in 45 *Congressional Globe* 1410, 2246, 3316, 4188, and in the *Appendix*, pp. 607–626 (1872); in 46 ibid., 1214, 1407 (1873); and in 2 *Congressional Record* 31, 38, 41, 45, 76, 164 (1873).

and that a member of the Senate cannot be unseated for bribery, because he cannot be indicted and punished for it in a court.[45]

The Senate, he declared, may only inquire whether a member meets the constitutional qualifications for his office, and it may expel a member only for his misconduct while serving in the Senate.

The committee's report left little doubt that the Senate was convinced it could judge such matters as bribery and corruption in obtaining election. Typically, however, Caldwell's case did not present—as far as various senators were concerned—clearly defined issues. There were the troublesome issues of *ex parte* proceedings and the absence of substantial evidence of wrongdoing. But there were senators, such as Carl Schurz, who did not doubt that the Senate could act. Bribery, said Schurz, is so "intimately connected with [one's] becoming and being a Senator that the two . . . cannot be separated; that therefore this power to expel a member must necessarily apply."[46]

The committee resolution declared that Caldwell was not "duly and legally elected"; but Senator Ferry proposed that Caldwell be expelled. There was, of course, a great difference between these proposals. If the Senate acted in accord with the committee resolution, it would have had to declare the seat vacant by reason of an invalid election. Expulsion, on the other hand, would imply a valid claim to membership, since this power can be exercised only against a sitting member. But no action was needed on either resolution, as Caldwell resigned on March 24, three days after Ferry introduced his resolution.[47]

Between 1873 and 1880 the Senate had to consider similar (and additional) charges against senators from Missouri, Arkansas, Oregon, and Kansas. Cases involving senators from Missouri and Arkansas were before the Senate at the same time as that of the Caldwell case, and, as in the latter, charges were brought that L. V. Bogy had obtained election by corrupt means. Senator Bogy claimed that a state legislative committee had investigated these charges but had found no evidence that would incriminate him. On March 18, 1873, a memorial from residents of Missouri again

---

[45] 1 *Congressional Record* 31 (1873).
[46] Ibid., p. 86.
[47] Ibid., p. 164.

raised the issue. Although Bogy still felt that he had been exonerated (as indicated by documents he read into the *Congressional Record*) a Senate inquiry was initiated.[48] On March 25 the committee reported that a memorial signed by thirty-seven members of the Missouri legislature alleged that Bogy had obtained election through bribery. The committee concluded, however, that no evidence other than what had been compiled by the Missouri House of Representatives had been introduced, and that this was not substantial enough to warrant further investigation. The committee's proposal that it be discharged was approved, thereby ending the Bogy case.[49]

Simultaneously, an inquiry into charges against Powell Clayton of Arkansas produced a divided committee—the majority claiming that the evidence was insufficient. One of the charges against Clayton was that his election to the Senate had been obtained by fraudulent means. According to affidavits of residents of Arkansas, Clayton and others had been indicted by a grand jury for fraudulence in a previous congressional election. Although Judge Boles had won a majority of the votes in the Third Congressional District, Clayton, who was governor at that time, had given the certificate of election to General Edwards. This indictment, obtained under a national law of 1870, reported that Clayton gave the certificate to Edwards, a Democrat, so that the governor could get Democratic support for his election to the Senate.

In the estimation of Senator Norwood, various indications of wrong-doing in obtaining election (bribery, making appointments as part of a political deal, and granting state aids to railroads in which legislators and their friends had interests) amply supported the charges against Clayton.[50] In his lengthy report to the Senate, Norwood sought to substantiate seven specific charges of misconduct by Clayton, but was unable to counter the majority's claim that the evidence was insufficient. Indeed, a number of senators refused to vote on the Clayton matter, contending they had had no opportunity to weigh the evidence. Although thirty-three senators voted for the majority

---

[48] 1 *Congressional Record* 102 (1873).

[49] Ibid., p. 182.

[50] 1 *Congressional Record* 176–182 (1873). Norwood presented a minority report.

report and only six voted against it, Powell Clayton's seat in the Senate may well have been upheld because many senators either were absent or declined to vote.[51]

In 1877 the Senate was faced with a unique case that involved Lafayette Grover of Oregon. His colleague, Senator Mitchell, presented a petition from residents of Oregon who claimed that bribery and corruption attended Grover's election, and stated that, as governor in 1876, he had participated in a scheme to deprive the state of its proper electoral vote in the Hayes-Tilden presidential contest. It was also charged that Grover had given false testimony before a Senate committee with respect to having certified a defeated candidate as a presidential elector. On the basis of these charges, the petitioners requested that Grover be denied membership in the Senate.[52]

The case arose while the senate was meeting in special session; Grover was given the oath of office; and about ten days later the Committee on Privileges and Elections was instructed to investigate the charges against him. A subcommittee then went to Oregon to obtain testimony, and later that year, on December 14, 1877, a resolution was adopted for printing the testimony; but no other action was taken in that session or the next (December 1878 to March 1879).

After charges of electoral bribery and corruption were raised against John J. Ingalls of Kansas in February 1880, a committee investigated and advised the Senate that its testimony proved the charges against Ingalls. However, the report stated, it could not be shown that enough votes had been fraudulently obtained to affect the outcome of Ingall's election. Nor could it be proved that Ingalls had been involved. If anything, the committee said, it appeared that the corrupt practices had been directed against his election rather than in his behalf.[53]

Because the foregoing cases could be said to follow from the Senate's power to judge the election and returns of its members, there probably was no need for insertion of the constitutional question about the breadth of the Senate's power. But since certain issues in these and the following cases were not related to

---

[51] Thirty-three senators did not vote. Ibid., p. 192.

[52] Ibid., 22–23 (1877).

[53] Ibid., 938 (1880).

election, returns, and constitutional qualifications, the mere act of investigating them provided an even wider base of precedents for subsequent actions.

In 1893 the Senate investigated charges against a member-elect from North Dakota whose offense had occurred long before his election and bore no relationship to it. A news item of March 15, 1893, charged that Senator Roach had embezzled funds while employed as a cashier in a bank many years earlier in the District of Columbia. Roach had embezzled $64,000, the news story claimed, and then fled to the Territory of North Dakota. (The Bank recovered some of the money from bondsmen and by attaching Roach's property in the District.) Because of the newspaper's charge, Senator Hoar of Massachusetts proposed that the Committee on Privileges and Elections make an investigation and that the Senate be informed of its duty. The constitutional question was at issue because the allegations pertained to an act of misconduct committed approximately fifteen years before Roach's election. Commenting on the constitutional question, Roach stated that various senators had informed him the Senate was powerless to act under the circumstances. This led to a debate in which Senators contended either that they had no power to judge a man's conduct before his election, or that they had to act in order to protect the integrity of the Senate. For all the flurry and debate it caused, this matter came to naught, and on April 15, 1893, this special session of the Senate ended. Although Senator Hansbrough of North Dakota worked for adoption of a resolution to investigate, the rules required unanimity and the Democrats were able to prevent action.[54]

Although no action was taken on Hansbrough's proposal, this case is an excellent portrayal of the role of precedents. In support of their claim that the Senate could investigate Roach for misconduct before he became a member, Senators Platt and Chandler made much of the several cases they considered apposite—those of Humphrey Marshall of Kentucky, Rice of Minnesota, and Stark of Oregon. There seemed to be a relationship between the Roach matter, and the Rice and Stark cases, but—at least in the

---

[54] Relevant information, resolutions, and debates are found in 25 *Congressional Record*, 37, 111, 138–160, 189 (1893).

debate—the pertinency of the Marshall case was in doubt. The only clear statement that issued from the Marshall case was that the Senate did *not* have jurisdiction. Yet Platt and Chandler emphasized the points that had been made in the Marshall case (for example, there had been no conviction and for this reason the Senate had refused to take jurisdiction) but failed to acknowledge the specific grounds upon which the Senate had disposed of that earlier matter.

The Democrats' arguments were equally irrelevant. Senator Mills cited the Trumbull case in arguing that neither the states nor Congress may add to the constitutional qualifications. Since the states may "not add to the qualifications of the servants they choose to represent them," he said, "certainly the Federal Congress to which they are sent can not do it, and if both branches can not do it by law, neither one can do it."[55]

The Trumbull case had not resulted in such a declaration; as we noted earlier, four different positions were expounded by the Senate. (1) Some senators claimed that a state may add qualifications, as in prohibiting the election to another office of a man who holds a state judicial post. (2) Others said that a state may add qualifications but that the Illinois constitutional limitation on state judges did not apply to Trumbull, because he had resigned his judgeship about eighteen months before he was elected to the Senate. (3) Both the states and the Congress may add to the qualifications, Stuart of Michigan argued, but these additional requirements must be contained in statutes to prevent arbitrary uses of this power. (4) Senator Butler of South Carolina declared that each chamber, not the states, had the power to make broad judgments about the fitness of a member—"to kick the scoundrel away from the door rather than admit him and then kick him out." But none of these positions had emerged as a specific policy statement of a majority of the senators. Therefore, Mills was wrong on this count. He was also wrong because Congress had prescribed additional statutory disqualifications since 1790 and because men had been denied membership on a number of occasions because of prior acts of misconduct.

So erratic were the practices of each chamber after 1870 that the House or the Senate could thereafter go in virtually any

[55] Ibid., p. 160.

direction. The precedents were sufficiently numerous and diverse to permit great selectivity. Moreover, when a Senate rule could operate to the benefit of the minority party (as in the Roach case), partisan considerations could dictate the most expedient course of action and the most suitable precedents.

VI

Twentieth-Century Cases: Crystallization of an
Answer to the Constitutional Question

Polygamy, corruption, racism, loyalty, and patriotism—and
congressmen serving time in penitentiaries instead of legislative
chambers—were features of the sensational cases of the twentieth
century. They were great enough in number and diverse enough
in the questions they raised to provide each house almost every
opportunity to consider the scope of its constitutional power.
Inevitably, there were those who challenged a chamber's action
by claiming that the power to judge the qualifications and conduct of its members was not as great as other congressmen
asserted. However, the majority now believed that the House and
Senate were not confined to matters of age, citizenship, and
inhabitancy. Consequently, the refusal to seat Roberts, Bilbo, and
Powell; the prolonged deliberations in the Smoot and Langer
cases; and the investigations into charges of misconduct before a
member's election demonstrate how definite the answer to the
constitutional question had become.

Although corruption in the electoral process and other forms
of misconduct figured prominently in these cases, they were not
the only matters that concerned the House and Senate. For
example, his opposition to America's entry into World War I was

the reason for Victor Berger's exclusion from the house on two occasions, and a "dovish" speech made Robert M. LaFollette the object of a censure move in the Senate.

The foregoing suggests the diversity of the issues that arose in twentieth-century cases. The disposition of some cases also reveals the greater certainty with which each chamber acted on extra-constitutional grounds. Equally revealing is the extent to which inconsistencies can be found. A consistent application of standards has been no more a virtue of the House or Senate in the twentieth century than it was in the nineteenth. Such inconsistencies not only underscore the arbitrariness with which the power to judge has been exercised but further demonstrate the need for clearly defined guidelines to assure that democratic principles are not sacrificed to partisan whim and capriciousness.

Constitutional Qualifications

Throughout the nineteenth century there were few instances in which the constitutional qualifications of age, citizenship, and inhabitancy and the second-office prohibition were in question. The same has been true in this century. Only the disqualification provided by the Fourteenth Amendment, inhabitancy, and holding a second office could have commanded—or did command—the attention of the House or Senate. And only one constitutional provision, the disability clause of the Fourteenth Amendment, was strictly applied. How differently constitutional tests were applied in the twentieth century becomes apparent in an examination of various situations pertinent to Victor Berger, Lyndon Baines Johnson, Pierre Salinger, and Robert Kennedy.

Because Berger, a Socialist, had served one term in the House of Representatives (1911 to 1913), this service later permitted the House to use the Fourteenth Amendment's disability provision against him. As a member of Congress, he had taken an oath to support the Constitution of the United States, which his critics claimed he violated by speaking against America's entry and involvement in World War I. These activities led to his conviction for violation of the Espionage Act of 1917, and were equated with giving "aid or comfort to the enemies" of the United States. Citing the Fourteenth Amendment, the House justified its denial of membership to Berger. This course of action, which revealed the continuing usefulness of the Fourteenth Amendment, created a precedent that could also be used in the case of another dovish congressman-elect.

Although the disability provision helped the House accomplish its end in the Berger case, the statements of various members leave little doubt that he would have been excluded even if the Fourteenth Amendment had not been applicable. One leader of the anti-Berger forces, Representative F. W. Dallinger of Massachusetts, contended there was an unbroken line of similar precedents to support a denial of membership. But even if there was no precedent, Dallinger continued, "now would be the time, and this is the place, for the House to make a new precedent."[1] Representative Joseph Eagle of Texas claimed that the specified qualifications in the Constitution did not preclude others. As judge of the election, returns, and qualifications of its members, the House "may ascertain whether there be other disqualifications." Eagle's examples of other disqualifications were insanity and an "infectious, odious disease."[2]

After a lengthy debate, the House voted Berger's exclusion on November 10, 1919, but Berger was returned in a special election and on January 10, 1920, presented a new set of credentials. Once more the House refused to seat him. Berger was elected a third time, in 1922, and in 1923 was seated without a challenge. His seating involved more than a change of heart in the house or a belated response to the popular will. At the time Berger had presented his credentials in 1919 and 1920, an appeal was pending against his conviction under the Espionage Act. And although in 1919 the Supreme Court had upheld the convictions of other Socialist-pacifists (Debs and Frohwerk) it overturned Berger's conviction in 1921, declaring the trial judge had been prejudiced. The government then decided not to bring Berger to trial again. Thus exonerated, Berger was more acceptable to the House of Representatives.

Instances that involved questions about the specific constitutional tests were handled in quite a different manner. Indeed, Congress was no longer asking the same kinds of questions it had

---

[1] 58 *Congressional Record* 8703 (1919).
[2] Ibid., p. 8969.

in the past. For one thing, the second-office prohibition was not as significant as it once had been. If the House and the Senate had applied the precedents of the John P. Van Ness (1802) and William Vandever (1863) cases, Lyndon Johnson would not have continued to be a representative while serving on active duty in the navy during World War II and Senator Goldwater and other members of Congress would not have been permitted to hold reserve commissions in the armed forces. The second-office prohibition and fear that the executive branch might unduly influence Congress were no longer matters of concern, as is reflected in the failure of the House and Senate to act even though these situations seemed to warrant action.

During World War II, Johnson and others were granted leaves of absence to serve in the armed forces, and their recall from military or naval service to their legislative duties was a consequence of presidential rather than congressional action. "Upon entry into [military] service," Attorney General Biddle advised President Roosevelt, "the individual ceases to be a Member of Congress, provided the House or Senate, as the case may be, chooses to act."[3] Apparently it was more important to President Roosevelt that young New Dealers be available in Congress to support his legislative proposals than on the battlefields fighting the enemy.

The meaning of the inhabitancy requirement was questioned in August 1964 when Pierre Salinger was appointed to fill the short-term vacancy created by the death of Senator Clair Engle of California. And by seating Salinger the Senate also cleared the way for Robert Kennedy in New York. In 1964 neither Salinger nor Kennedy was eligible to vote in their own elections. Yet each was a candidate for the Senate. There was, therefore, serious doubt about the eligibility of each man when each appeared to take the oath of office.

In 1964 Salinger had won the Democratic primary in California; consequently, upon the death of Senator Engle, the Democratic governor appointed Salinger to fill the vacancy. Immediately upon presenting his credentials, Salinger was challenged. The Republicans (including their California nominee for the

---

[3] 40 *Opinions of the Attorneys General* (ed. John T. Fowler) 301–302 (1949).

Senate, George Murphy) were apparently concerned that incumbency might give Salinger an advantage in the general election of 1964. In waging their battle against Salinger, the Republicans advanced two principal arguments. The first pertained to the constitutional definition of inhabitancy; the second derived from a statutory requirement in California. Since Salinger was not an eligible voter in California, having moved there from Virginia only shortly before the primary election in June, he did not seem to be an inhabitant within the meaning of the constitutional requirement. Also, a California statute stipulated that an appointee must be an elector, which means a person must have been a resident of the state for at least a year.

It was possible, of course, for the Senate to reject this state requirement, as it had done in the Trumbull case more than a century before. However, this precedent was not the controlling argument, for the Seventeenth Amendment permits each state legislature to "empower the executive thereof (i.e. the governor) to make temporary appointments until the people fill the vacancies by election as the legislature may direct." Some senators believed this grant of authority was broad enough to override California's statutory requirement that an appointee be an elector. If the Constitution's inhabitancy requirement was strictly construed, a United States Senator, whether elected or appointed, would be presumed to be a qualified voter of the state he represented. Certainly the California statute was based upon such a presumption.

After extensive debate, Salinger was given the oath of office without prejudice; the question of his eligibility was then submitted to the Committee on Rules and Administration. On August 13, 1964, the committee reported that (1) a senator is not bound by state requirements as long as he meets the tests of the United States Constitution, and (2) the Senate is the sole and exclusive judge of the qualifications of its members-elect.[4] After further debate, the Senate decided that Salinger was entitled to membership.

Although this was a fleeting victory for Salinger, who was defeated by Murphy the following November, it cleared the way for Robert Kennedy, whose election as senator from New York

---

[4] 110 *Congressional Record* 18107, 19396 (1964).

also was marred by the inhabitancy requirement. When he presented his credentials in January 1965, no challenge was forthcoming. The Senate seemed satisfied that the inhabitancy requirement was met if a member-elect was a resident of the state he represented at the time of his election.

Thus the Berger case showed the potential of section 3 of the Fourteenth Amendment. The Salinger decision provided at least a partisan answer to the meaning of inhabitancy. And, in their failure to act on second-office cases, both chambers disregarded the reason for which this prohibition had been incorporated in Article I of the Constitution. However, the many other instances in which the House and Senate acted on extra-constitutional grounds were much more significant.

Again, as in the nineteenth century, these cases fall into several categories. The first category covers members-elect whose alleged misconduct had occurred prior to their election. In some cases the allegations pertained to incidents prior to their first election—indeed, even many years in advance of election. A second type of cases is those in which no action was taken until after a member's reelection, even though the alleged offenses were committed during a previous term as congressman. Finally, there are several cases in which members of Congress were charged with misconduct committed during a current session.

The chambers did not act against the wrongdoers in every instance. Sometimes they left the responsibility for determining whether felonies had been committed to the Department of Justice and federal courts. The important point is that on every occasion in which the House and Senate acted, the power of a chamber to judge its members on extra-constitutional grounds was further solidified.

The Polygamy Cases

At the outset of the twentieth century the House had a new opportunity to consider the scope of its power over members-elect. Brigham Roberts, a Mormon and a polygamist, had been elected to Utah's seat in the House of Representatives, and when Roberts presented his credentials (December 4, 1899), Representative Taylor of Ohio objected to the oath being given. There were several reasons for Taylor's action. In 1889, Roberts had been convicted of polygamy. Furthermore, since Roberts still lived in a polygamous arrangement, Taylor contended, he was disqualified by the Edmunds Act of 1882—"and for higher and graver and quite as sound reasons."[5] Finally, Taylor reminded his colleagues of the petitions signed by seven million Americans who objected to the seating of Representative-elect Roberts.

These were ample grounds for denying membership to Roberts, Taylor argued. Roberts had been convicted and sentenced to a four-month jail term for violating the antipolygamy statute, the Edmunds Act, which disqualified polygamists for public office. Roberts, moreover, had been a lawbreaker ever since that time inasmuch as he was still married to more than one woman. And, Taylor claimed, each house may judge a member-elect on grounds other than those of age, citizenship, and inhabitancy.

It was on this occasion that a different meaning was given to the "negative argument" voiced by Representative Randolph almost a century earlier, an argument Randolph devised to support his claim that states may add to the qualifications. The only limitation on states' power, Randolph had declared, was that a member-elect could not be less than twenty-five, an alien, or a transient. Now, in Taylor's hands, this negative argument was used to support a broad authority in Congress.

And that clause of the Constitution was most ably and ingeniously and persuasively argued in 1807 upon the floor of the House of Representatives by John Randolph. I think no man can read that argument without being convinced at least as to the power of Congress.[6]

Roberts, however, had support from some of the members of the House who believed that this power to judge qualifications was limited and who were concerned about the implications of a broad-based power for democracy. Nevertheless, the spokesmen and the votes on his behalf were few.

The case for Roberts, as he and others presented it, was based on three points. First, a sovereign state has the right to be represented, and a member-elect who presents valid credentials has a right to be given the oath of office. Second (as Roberts reminded the House), after Utah's admission to the Union presidential amnesties had been given to all men who had been

---

[5] 33 ibid., 5 (1899).
[6] Ibid., p. 39.

disqualified by the Edmunds Act. Finally, how could Roberts be labeled a persistent lawbreaker and yet not be punished for breaking the law?[7]

After a lengthy debate on these points, Taylor's resolution was adopted. Roberts was denied the oath until such time as a special committee had investigated him and made a recommendation on the disposition of his case. On January 23, 1900, majority and minority reports were presented to the House, but all members of the committee agreed that Roberts was a polygamist. The minority, nevertheless, declared that Roberts had been duly elected and should be given the oath of office. It also recommended that Roberts be expelled since, as a polygamist, his was an unlawful status.

Presumably, the minority position conformed to a strict construction of the Constitution, to the belief that the House could not judge a member-elect on any grounds other than those specified by the Constitution. But the minority noted that the House could not be prevented from acting later. As a polygamist, Roberts was in violation of the law, and as a sworn member of Congress, his conduct could be judged.

Although it had more than the required two-thirds vote to expel Roberts, the House adopted the majority report, which concluded that Roberts should not be seated. After further debate, in which both sides used and abused precedents, the minority report was rejected 244 to 81. The House then denied membership to Roberts by a vote of 268 to 50.[8] For a combination of reasons—his conviction as a polygamist, his disqualification under the Edmunds Act, and his continuous status as a polygamist—the House felt justified in denying Roberts membership.

Several years later the Senate was confronted with the polygamy issue deciding whether Reed Smoot of Utah was eligible for membership. But Smoot, an elder of the Mormon Church, was not a polygamist, had not been convicted of violating an antipolygamy statute, and had not been rendered ineligible by any national law. Only in one respect can the Smoot case be compared to Roberts's: their claims to membership were opposed not only by many members of Congress but by religious organiza-

---

[7] See the arguments of Representative Richardson and Brigham Roberts in ibid., pp. 43, 47 (1899).

[8] Ibid., pp. 1216–1217 (Jan. 25, 1900).

tions throughout the United States. Indeed, in initiating an action against Smoot, Senator Boies Penrose called his colleagues' attention to the many petitions that had been received from religious groups. In the more than three years the case was before the Senate, additional petitions were constantly received, all demanding that Smoot be excluded.

Since Smoot was a monogamist, it is not readily apparent why his right to membership should have been questioned, but a partial answer was provided by Senator Shelby Cullom of Illinois and by the committee that investigated Smoot: "If the hierarchy of the Mormon Church exists as it once existed," Cullom wrote in 1905;

if it penetrates, as it once penetrated, into the affairs of citizenship; if it dictates, as it once dictated, courses of conduct at variance with the laws of the land under whose flag it claims protection and privilege—then it is a menace, and it is high time that we demanded reformation.[9]

Most of the committee members shared this judgment.

The most critical point in the majority report was the fact that Smoot was one of the fifteen elders who constituted "the ruling authorities of the Church of Jesus Christ of the Latter Day Saints." This ruling body, which claimed to be the supreme authority of the church, the report said, passes judgment upon all matters, civil and religious. By "uniting in themselves authority in church and state, these elders do so exercise the same as to inculcate and encourage a belief in polygamy and polygamous habitation."[10] By exercising spiritual and secular powers, the committee claimed, this governing authority also violated the principle of separation of church and state. Although Smoot was a monogamist, the majority claimed that by reason of his position in the church he "encourages, counsels, and approves polygamy"—conduct that fell within the legal definition of a conspiratorial act. Finally, the report referred to an "oath of vengeance." According to testimony taken by the committee, those who took this oath promised "to avenge the blood of the prophets upon this nation." The provisions of the oath were taught to young chil-

---

[9] "The Menace of Mormonism," 181 *North American Review* 379 (1905).

[10] 40 *Congressional Record* 8219 (1906).

dren, witnesses claimed, together with a prayer that the murder of Joseph Smith, the founder of Mormonism, would be avenged.

For these several reasons—the violation of the principle of separation of church and state, conduct of a conspiratorial nature, and the alleged oath of vengeance—a majority of the commitee recommended that Smoot be declared ineligible for membership.[11]

The minority took issue with each of these arguments and claimed that Smoot was constitutionally qualified to be a senator. Smoot was not a polygamist, the minority reported; moreover, it was well known that he was opposed to polygamy. The minority also reminded the Senate that the religious beliefs of Smoot and his church were protected by the Constitution of the United States. And there was a serious doubt about the so-called oath of vengeance, the minority contended; credible witnesses had denied there was such a thing and that its alleged provisions were part of Mormon teaching. Finally, the minority took a position toward polygamy that coincided with the implicit policy of the national government: it should be permitted to disappear gradually with the older generations of Mormons. The only alternative, wholesale prosecution of polygamists, would lead to serious social problems, inasmuch as large numbers of women and children would be deprived of a breadwinner.[12]

No action was immediately taken on either the majority or minority recommendations, and when Congress reconvened in December 1906 it was again flooded with petitions from religious organizations. On December 11, the Senate began debate on the majority recommendation that Smoot be declared ineligible for membership, and the case was resolved on February 20, 1907, more than three years after Smoot had been given the oath of office. The Senate adopted an amendment to the majority report: *Resolved* (two-thirds of the Senators present concurring therein), that Reed Smoot is not entitled." By adopting this amendment the Senate indicated that the situation required expulsion rather than exclusion. In effect, then, the Senate was judging

---

[11] Ibid., p. 8223. The majority report is found in ibid., pp. 8216–8226.

[12] Ibid., pp. 8226–8238. Serious social problems had also been foreseen by Brigham Young almost forty years earlier.

Smoot's conduct at the present time rather than his acts or beliefs before the time of his election. However, this effort to make it more difficult to remove Smoot from the Senate was not needed, since the resolution to declare him ineligible had not received even majority support.[13]

By conducting an investigation into the charges against Smoot, the Senate—by implication—claimed broad authority, and thus the Smoot case could be claimed as such a precedent on later occasions. For example, even though the Constitution forbids a religious test as a condition for holding national office, Smoot had been judged on the grounds of his religious association and beliefs. If the Senate could judge a member-elect on these grounds, what could prevent it from judging another member or member-elect by his political associations and beliefs?

Misconduct before Election

On December 6, 1926, when Arthur R. Gould appeared in the Senate to take the oath, Senator Thomas Walsh of Montana raised a question about an allegation of misconduct reported by a judge in a Canadian court. According to a press account, which Walsh included in a resolution calling for a committee investigation of Gould, the judge

in a formal opinion found and charged that a contract made on the basis of [judicial] proceedings was tainted with bribery perpetrated by or participated in by Arthur R. Gould, certified to have been elected a Senator from the State of Maine.[14]

Only the next day, after Walsh's resolution was taken up by the Senate, did it become apparent that the alleged bribery incident had occurred fourteen years before Gould's election. Gould's colleague from Maine, Senator Hale, reported that this same charge had been made during the election campaign, and said that the voters of the state had dismissed it by electing Gould.

Because of the time factor, there was some uncertainty about investigating the charge against Gould. Indeed, said Senator Reed, such an investigation was beyond the jurisdiction of the

---

[13] 41 ibid., 3428–3429 (1907).
[14] 68 ibid., 8–9 (1926).

Senate; nor could the Senate claim jurisdiction because of Gould's willingness to have the charge investigated. However, the Senate adopted Walsh's resolution by an overwhelming vote, 70 to 7. Almost three months later, the Committee on Privileges and Elections recommended that Gould be declared entitled to membership.[15]

In the Langer case in 1941, allegations of misconduct dated back to 1914. When Langer presented himself as a senator-elect on January 3, 1941, Senate Majority Leader Barkley reported that objections had been filed by citizens of North Dakota. These charges were alarming, Barkley said, and if they were true they "would seriously affect the qualifications and fitness of the Senator-elect to become a member of this body."[16] It was then agreed that Langer would be given the oath of office "without prejudice," but his tenure in the Senate would depend upon the outcome of a committee investigation. "Without prejudice" also meant, Barkley explained, that if the charges were proved, Langer could be removed by a simple majority vote rather than expelled by a two-thirds vote. Not until March 27, 1942, was there a decision on Langer's eligibility. The Senate voted down two parts of a committee recommendation that declared him "not to be entitled to be a Senator of the United States from the State of North Dakota."[17]

The majority of the committee, with Scott Lucas of Illinois acting as spokesman, believed there were ample grounds for excluding Langer. Lucas agreed that it was not fair to take isolated instances of misconduct a score or more years ago, but, he told his colleagues, it was proper to consider "a pattern made up of one case after another over a long period of time, culminating in the case we are now discussing." The charges of moral turpitude against Langer, Lucas claimed, "have woven themselves into a pattern of moral turpitude up to 1940."[18]

These charges were of various kinds. One was that Langer's election had been obtained by fraudulent means—"the casting and counting in his favor of, to wit, many thousands of illegal absentee ballots," and the destruction of thousands of valid bal-

---

[15] Ibid., p. 5914 (1967).
[16] 87 ibid., 3 (1941).
[17] Ibid., 3063–3064 (1942).
[18] Ibid., p. 2175.

lots. The petitioners also claimed that in the previous twenty years Langer's

public and private life has been of such character that he has been repeatedly suspected and accused of conduct involving moral turpitude.

Reportedly, Langer had (1) been recalled as governor of North Dakota; (2) admitted in a federal court that he received $19,000 in kickback money from state and national employees and state contractors; (3) bribed two jurors; (4) received $4,000 for issuing a pardon; (5) benefited in the amount of $75,000 from the purchase and sale of county bonds; (6) obtained a kickback of $976 from the purchase of road equipment; and (7) procured a client's temporary release from jail, taken him across state lines, and got the man remarried so that his wife could not testify against him.

After all such charges were investigated, the committee majority recommended:

Resolved, That the case of William Langer does not fall within the constitutional provisions for expulsion by a two-thirds vote.

Resolved, That William Langer is not entitled to be a Senator of the United States from the State of North Dakota.

The first part of this recommendation was defeated 45 to 37; the second part was rejected 52 to 30.

Ample opportunity had been afforded each side to debate the extent of the Senate's power to judge its members. As on other occasions—dating back to the Niles case in the 1840s and even to Humphrey Marshall's case in 1796—the mere act of taking jurisdiction and conducting an investigation suggests that the senators believed their power to judge had broad dimensions.

The Langer case also gave the Senate another opportunity to consider the merits of Randolph's negative argument, this time as justification for a chamber's going beyond the specific requirements of the Constitution. The age, citizenship, and inhabitancy qualifications are minimal, Senator George of Georgia claimed. Over and beyond these qualifications

is the whole broad field of whether, in the opinion of the Senate itself, the necessary qualifications are found to exist, and if they are found not to exist and the Senate is persuaded that matters of such gravity are involved as to impel its action in excluding one who comes here with a certificate, I have not any doubt that we will have the full power to act.[19]

Contrary arguments were offered by Senators Connally and Murdoch, both of whom rejected the negative argument and objected to the Senate's going beyond the specific requirements of the Constitution.

That the decision to seat Langer embraced more than one position seems obvious from the record. Connally, Murdoch, and others voted for Langer in the belief that the Senate's power is not as great as the committee claimed. For others, the time factor was most important. The senators also weighed the fact that, although Langer had been convicted in a federal court, his conviction had been overturned on appeal; and although the voters of North Dakota had recalled him as their governor, they had later chosen him to be their senator. The Senate also believed it should not act in a case where the evidence was unsubstantial or was based on hearsay—and apparently the evidence against Langer was not considered sufficient for seeking indictments and bringing him to trial.

These were compelling reasons for voting against the committee's recommendation that Langer be declared ineligible, and strong enough to justify the Senate's vote to seat Langer. We can scarcely claim, therefore, that the Senate's decision in the Langer case signified that it had repudiated precedents and limited itself to judging the age, citizenship, and inhabitancy qualifications of a member. Indeed, by refusing to give the oath of office to Theodore Bilbo of Mississippi in 1947, the Senate again claimed a power as broad as the power defined by Senator George in the Langer case.

Corrupters of the Electoral Process

Langer's was only one of several notable cases in the late nineteenth and early twentieth centuries in which charges of election fraud were made against senators-elect. A rich man who wanted to buy a public office for himself looked "first to the Senate," said the editor of *Outlook* in 1907, because he knew

---

[19] 88 ibid., 2390 (1942).

"that whereas a whole State may not be purchasable, a Legislature may be."[20] "Togas for sale," the phrase with which Robert and Leona Rienow described the rich man's acquisition of a seat in the United States Senate, was one of the reasons for the adoption of the Seventeenth Amendment. From 1789 to 1913, state legislatures elected United States senators, but because of the frequent charges that they were corrupted by selling Senate seats to the highest bidder, the Progressives initiated a campaign that eventuated in the Seventeenth Amendment and the direct, popular election of senators.

Presumably, democracy had been served and corruption was brought to an end when the Seventeenth Amendment took effect in 1913. Unfortunately, however, even after the adoption of this amendment, there were charges that elections had been rigged. Four such cases were those of William Lorimer of Illinois, Truman Newberry of Michigan, William Vare of Pennsylvania, and Frank Smith of Illinois. The Lorimer case arose before the adoption of the Seventeenth Amendment; the latter three cases arose after its adoption, and seemed to disprove the claim of the editor of *Outlook:* a rich man could purchase a whole state as well as the state legislature.[21]

At the time the direct election amendment was being ratified by the state legislatures, the charge was made that Senator Lorimer had obtained his election by bribery and corruption. A member of the Illinois House of Representatives, Charles A. White, said he had been bribed to vote for Lorimer, and he agreed to sell the story of the election fraud to the *Chicago Tribune.* The United States Senate thereupon adopted a resolution (on June 20, 1910) that called for an investigation. After taking evidence in Illinois, the Committee on Privileges and Elections reported there was no substance to White's claims. Possibly, the committee reported, four state legislators had been bribed; however, since Lorimer had been elected by a fourteen-vote margin, corruption on so small a scale could not have

---

[20] Quoted by Robert Rienow and Leona T. Rienow in *Of Snuff, Sin and the Senate,* p. 110 (1965).

[21] These three or four cases were only the most sensational cases that arose after the direct, popular election of senators was instituted. For a study of other electoral cases both before and after the adoption of the Seventeenth Amendment, see *Of Snuff, Sin and the Senate,* chap. 10: "Togas for Sale" (1965).

affected the outcome. The committee also stated that, although several state legislators had been indicted for corrupt practices, none had been convicted. Moreover, "most of the men charged with crime and corruption have been reelected to office by the people of Illinois."[22]

The verdicts of the courts and the people of Illinois carried enough weight among senators to give Lorimer a narrow margin of support in Washington. By a vote of 46 to 40, the Senate turned down the resolution of the Progressives (LaFollette and Beveridge) that Lorimer be declared "not duly and legally elected."

In the long run, however, the Progressive forces won out. On May 18, 1911, slightly more than two months after the resolution was defeated, the Illinois Senate declared that Lorimer's election had been obtained by corrupt means. When a copy of the state senate's resolution was received by the United States Senate, a new investigation was ordered. More than a year later, on July 13, 1912, the Senate adopted a committee recommendation and invalidated Lorimer's election by a vote of 55 to 28.[23] Thus Lorimer had the dubious distinction of being the last senator who was declared ineligible by reason of corrupting a state legislature.[24]

In the two decades that followed the adoption of the Seventeenth Amendment, charges of expenditures of vast sums of money and various corrupt practices were at issue in cases involving senators-elect from Michigan, New Hampshire, Texas, Illinois, and Pennsylvania. In three of these cases the defendants were either forced to resign because of the publicity (Newberry of Michigan) or were formally denied membership (Smith of

---

[22] The committee report is found in 46 *Congressional Record* 547–552 (1910).

[23] 48 ibid., 8968, 8987 (1912).

[24] Isaac Stephenson of Wisconsin almost shared this distinction. On June 29, 1911, the Senate received a joint resolution adopted by fifty-eight members of the Wisconsin General Assembly, and because of the charges of corruption contained therein a Senate investigation was undertaken. The committee majority was not convinced by the evidence but a five-man minority reported that $107,000 had been made available to run the election for Stephenson. On Mar. 27, 1912, the Senate voted in Stephenson's favor; however, the margin of victory (40 to 34) was so slight as to leave a reasonable doubt of his innocence (48 ibid., 3816 [1912]).

Illinois and Vare of Pennsylvania). However, Senators Moses of New Hampshire and Mayfield of Texas were able to retain their seats.

An investigation of Truman Newberry, the Republican senatorial candidate in Michigan in 1918, was demanded even before the general election was held. Newberry, who was then on active duty in the navy, was pitted against Henry Ford in the Republican primary, and Ford was also enrolled in the Democratic primary, which he won. In effect, then, the general election in November was a re-match between two primary contenders. But so much derogatory information had been made public through disclosures about the amount of money spent in Newberry's behalf during the primary election that Republicans were fearful about the outcome of the general election. Indeed, when Senator Atlee Pomerene, a Democrat from Ohio, introduced a resolution in September 1918 demanding an investigation into charges that the money spent in Newberry's primary campaign violated the corrupt practices law, the Republicans countered that this was no more than an effort to lessen Newberry's chances of winning the Senate seat.

Partisan considerations no doubt motivated the Democrats, yet Pomerene's resolution grew out of a letter the Republican lieutenant governor of Michigan, Dickinson, had written to Newberry. In this letter Dickinson informed the Republican candidate that an estimated $250,000 to $500,000 had been spent on his behalf in the primary campaign. He requested, moreover, that Newberry withdraw from the Senate race for the sake of the Republican Party, clean politics, the integrity of primary elections, and to preserve both the party and Michigan "from a pollution that would stay for years."[25]

Despite his adverse publicity, Newberry defeated Ford, who then challenged his right to be a member of the United States Senate. One of the elements in the ensuing election contest was the Corrupt Practices Act of 1910, by which Congress limited

---

[25] From a letter read into the *Congressional Record* at the time Pomerene introduced his resolution (56 ibid. 10386 [1918]). For a complete inquiry into all facets of this case, see Spencer Ervin, *Henry Ford vs. Truman H. Newberry: The Famous Senate Election Contest* (1935).

campaign expenditures in both primary and general elections. Although Newberry had been convicted of violating this statute, his conviction had been set aside by the Supreme Court in 1921 in a 5 to 4 decision. The power of Congress to regulate "the times, places, and manner of holding elections" does not extend to primary elections, the Court ruled.[26] Therefore, if Newberry's claim to membership were to be denied, it would be a consequence of the Senate's accepting the charges made by Henry Ford in contesting the general election.

Claiming to be the duly elected senator and requesting that Newberry be investigated by a Senate committee, Ford demanded that the vote be recounted. The election boards in almost all of Michigan's 2,200 precincts were controlled by Republicans, he declared, and they had not made an accurate count of the ballots. Ford also charged that the Newberry forces had spent excessive sums of money to influence both the primary and general elections. Finally, Ford charged Newberry's supporters with intimidating and unduly influencing the voters.[27]

An investigation of these charges was undertaken by the Committee on Privileges and Elections, and a subcommittee recounted all the available ballots. Since some precincts had destroyed the ballots, the original official counts were accepted; and the committee's majority concluded that Newberry had been the winner by 4,000 votes. With respect to excessive expenditures of money, the majority reported that this had been done without the connivance of Newberry, who did not reside in the state at the time of the primary election. Newberry's affidavits also helped sway the committee; he claimed that he had not been aware of how much money was spent on his behalf, that he had not sanctioned these expenditures, and that all the work on his behalf had been voluntarily undertaken in his absence.

For all the foregoing reasons, the committee recommended that Newberry be declared duly elected and qualified. However,

---

[26] Newberry et al. v. U.S., 256 U.S. 232 (1921). The "Newberry doctrine," which held that primary elections are not covered by the Corrupt Practices Act, was overruled by the Court in U.S. v. Classic, 313 U.S. 299 (1941).

[27] See the minority report in 61 *Congressional Record* 7746–7775 (1921).

the narrowness of the vote, 46 to 41, indicated widespread dissatisfaction over his campaign expenditures. Even the majority resolution reflected this concern:

That whether the amount expended in this primary was $195,000 as was fully reported or whether there were some few thousand dollars in excess, the amount expended was in either case too large, much larger than ought to have been expended.

The expenditure of such excessive sums in behalf of a candidate, either with or without his knowledge and consent, being contrary to sound public policy, harmful to the honor and dignity of the Senate, and dangerous to the perpetuity of a free government, such expenditures are hereby severely condemned and disapproved.[28]

Almost four years' time had been expended on the Newberry case, and although his right to membership was narrowly upheld in January 1922, the adverse publicity had been such as to compel his resignation less than a year later. On November 21, 1922, the Senate received a copy of Newberry's letter to the governor of Michigan in which he announced his resignation. In addition to the "partisan political persecution" that had affected his work as a senator, Newberry referred to the defeat of the senior senator from Michigan, Senator Townsend, in the election of 1922. The prolonged debate over his (Newberry's) right to membership had been responsible, he said, for Townsend's defeat.[29]

Fully as sensational and protracted were the cases against Senators-elect William S. Vare of Pennsylvania and Frank L. Smith of Illinois, which began June 26, 1926, with Senator Caraway's reference to the country's shock over the enormous expenditures of money in the Pennsylvania and Illinois primaries. Moreover, Caraway declared, Smith, the chairman of the Illinois Public Utilities Commission, had received large amounts of money from Samuel Insull, "the real utility monarch," and had won his primary election while retaining his post on the commission. And he intended, Caraway said, to retain his post on the commission throughout the campaign preceding the general election.

As in the Newberry case, reports of large expenditures in the

---

[28] 62 ibid., 1062 (1922).
[29] 63 ibid., 15 (1922).

primary elections were made in the Senate even before the general elections in November; thus Smith's and Vare's critics left themselves open to charges that they were attempting to influence the voters of Illinois and Pennsylvania. Indeed, Representative Garrett of Texas made such a plea directly to the Pennsylvania electorate. "Pennsylvania has now reached a position where it is the open shame of the Republic," he said, and he expressed the hope that the voters would "redeem" their state in the general election.[30]

These two cases, again like Newberry's, were unique in that so much of the groundwork for the senate's later action was laid in advance of the general elections, that is, before the appearance in chamber of Smith and Vare as senators-elect. A special committee investigation in 1926 reported that more than $800,000 had been expended in Vare's primary campaign and more than $400,000 in Smith's. There was the additional disclosure that Smith, whose official responsibilities included the regulation of public utilities, had received a $125,000 contribution from Insull, the public utilities tycoon.[31] Thus "progressive" forces prepared the way for the exclusion of Smith and Vare both before and after the general elections, providing the Senate with constant reminders about the charges against the two men. However, those who opposed the seating of Smith and Vare were unable to get Senate support for resolutions that would have declared each man ineligible in advance of March 4, 1927, when they would present their credentials to the new Congress.

Formal action against Smith, nevertheless, commenced before the new Congress met; because of a vacancy in the Senate, the governor of Illinois had appointed him to serve out the unexpired term. Thus on January 19, 1927, Senator Charles S. Deneen of Illinois presented Smith's credentials of appointment and a resolution calling for his seating and investigation of the charges against him.[32] Initially, the Senate's attention was focused on the extent and nature of its power and whether Smith should be given the oath "without prejudice to any subsequent proceeding

---

[30] Ibid. 13023 (1926).

[31] In December 1926, Senator Dill referred to these reports in proposing that neither man be seated on Mar. 4, 1927 (68 ibid. 119–120 [1926]).

[32] Ibid., p. 1911.

in this case." By a vote of 49 to 32, the Senate decided to withhold the oath until it had received a report and recommendation from the Committee on Privileges and Elections. Because of illness Smith was unable to appear before the committee, and its investigation of the charges against him was delayed.

At the end of the Sixty-ninth Congress, the committee reported that it could do no more than report upon Smith's credentials, which meant it could do no more than read his certificate. Thus determination of Smith's eligibility was now up to the Seventieth Congress, which also had to consider Vare's case.

Resolutions presented to the Seventieth Congress by Senator George Norris of Nebraska called for the exclusion of Smith and Vare. In addition to the charges already made against each man, Norris introduced a letter from Governor Pinchot of Pennsylvania that asserted Vare had not been honestly elected. According to Pinchot, "the stealing of votes for Mr. Vare and the amount and sources of the money spent in his behalf make it clear to me that the election returns do not in fact correctly represent the will of the sovereign voters of Pennsylvania."[33] Because the credentials of Smith and Vare were tainted by fraud and corruption, Norris said in his resolutions, neither man should be given the oath of office. Smith and Vare stood aside while the oath of office was administered to other senators-elect.

New investigations were initiated in December 1927, and the next month—on January 17, 1928, the committee stated its conviction that the charges against Smith had been substantiated. Therefore it concluded that he was not entitled to be a senator. On January 19, 1928, the Senate adopted a resolution that declared Smith was not entitled to membership.[34]

Not until December 1929 did the Senate adopt a resolution denying membership to Vare. This delay was caused by Vare's having suffered a paralytic stroke in the summer of 1928 and therefore he had been unable to appear before the committee. Since the committee was able to complete its investigation, the majority stated that the full Senate had to decide what should be done. In February 1929, Senators Robinson and Norris proposed that Vare be denied a seat; on the next day, however, Norris suggested that the resolution not be pressed: there should be a

---

[33] 69 ibid., 3–4 (1927).
[34] Ibid., p. 1718.

continuance because of Vare's ill health. In September, when the Senate had information that Vare had recovered, Senator Borah said there was no reason for a further delay and requested that Vare be denied membership. Nevertheless, the Senate voted to delay action until December. On December 3, Senator Norris again introduced a resolution to deny a seat to Vare and after several days of debate this resolution was adopted by a vote of 58 to 22.[35]

Misconduct by Members of Congress

When "Pitchfork Ben" Tillman and his fellow South Carolinian, Senator McLaurin, exchanged blows after the latter characterized a statement by Tillman as "a willful, malicious, and deliberate lie," the Senate immediately adopted a resolution holding the two men in contempt. Approximately one week later, although both men had apologized to the Senate to purge themselves of contempt, the Committee on Privileges and Elections recommended that they be censured. During the subsequent roll call, McLaurin said that for obvious reasons he could not vote, but Tillman said that "among gentlemen an apology for an offense committed under heat of blood is usually considered sufficient." Some of his colleagues regarded this as a new insult to the Senate. After Tillman withdrew his remarks, the President pro tem was able to assuage the ruffled tempers and bring the incident to an end.[36]

Twentieth-century representatives and senators were not as pugilistically inclined as their pre–Civil War counterparts; censure was a more common device for settling personal scores and legislative altercations. That censure, or an even more severe punishment, was not imposed upon Senator Robert LaFollette was not the fault of Pomerene and other like-minded senators, who believed LaFollette's comments regarding America's involvement in World War I were seditious and gave aid and comfort to the enemies of the United States. The situation warranted some kind of action, Senator Pomerene argued, whether it be censure, expulsion, or exoneration.

---

[35] 72 ibid., 197 (Dec. 6, 1929).
[36] 35 ibid. 2087–2089, 2206–2207 (1902).

In September 1917, when LaFollette spoke to the Nonpartisan League in St. Paul, Minnesota, the Wisconsin senator had attacked "flag-waving" corporations that, he said, were making a fortune from the war. He had likened the situation to the period of the Mexican War, when Abraham Lincoln and others had demanded the withdrawal of American troops. Surely, LaFollette told his audience, if Lincoln and the other war critics were nevertheless patriots, the most humble citizen had the right "to discuss freely the question of whether this war might not be terminated with honor" and to advocate an end to the "awful slaughter." The Minnesota Commission on Public Safety thereupon submitted documents and a petition to the Senate in calling for an investigation to decide whether LaFollette should be expelled for teaching "disloyalty and sedition," and for giving aid and comfort to America's enemies. The petition and copy of the speech were presented to the Senate on September 29, 1917, by Senator Frank Kellogg and an investigation by the Committee on Privileges and Elections was ordered.

When the committee reported on January 16, 1919, the majority report stated that nothing in LaFollette's speech warranted action by the Senate. It therefore recommended that the matter be dismissed. Chairman Pomerene, who presented the minority report, claimed the Senate had broad authority to judge the conduct of its members and, since it was obvious that LaFollette was guilty of disorderly conduct by reason of his seditious speech, a more extensive inquiry should be made to determine what course of action should be taken. Aside from a rather emotional appeal by Senator Williams, debate on the majority recommendation was limited, for it became obvious that the Senate was not anxious to become deeply involved. When the resolution to dismiss the case was put to a vote, it was adopted 50 to 21.[37]

The Senate's implicit decision not to censure LaFollette for his antiwar views was in sharp contrast to the House's handling of Victor Berger, who had earlier been convicted under the Espionage Act of 1917. Nevertheless, the latter had been convicted for public utterances and published statements that were no more serious in their denunciations and tone than LaFollette's.

---

[37] 57 ibid., 1506–1509, 1525–1527 (1919).

Leniency for Erring Members

Between 1924 and 1967, the disposition of cases in which serious charges were raised against members of Congress was anything but uniform. At times a chamber acted simultaneously with the Department of Justice, or the House or Senate deferred to the Attorney General, preferring that the disposition of a case be made in courts of law. And there were instances in which a chamber's action indicated that it did not much care whether a case presented an indictable offense. The two houses acted in so erratic a manner during this period of more than four decades that we can safely conclude only one thing: A chamber has discretionary power to decide how or whether it will act. However, the way in which it exercises this discretionary power necessarily leads to charges of inconsistency in the application of standards. To illustrate, we will examine several cases that arose between 1924 and 1967.

In 1924 an indictment against Senator Burton K. Wheeler was returned in the United States District Court of Montana on charges that grew out of a statute prohibiting members of Congress and other federal officials from receiving compensation for services rendered in any proceeding to which the United States was a party. This applied to cases being tried before civil courts and military tribunals.[38] Although the specific question was whether Wheeler had obtained compensation after his election to the Senate, this was by no means the precise problem with which the Senate had to contend; there were political implications in the charges. Wheeler and his Senate colleague from Montana, Thomas Walsh, were largely responsible for the Senate's investigations of the "Ohio Gang," including Attorney General Daugherty. Thus, Wheeler attributed the indictment to an effort by the Department of Justice to "get" him.[39]

In addition to the political events pertaining to this case were important questions about the specific intent of the statutory prohibition, inasmuch as Wheeler's law firm had represented a

---

[38] The charges are included in a report by Senator Borah, chairman of a select committee that investigated Wheeler, in 65 ibid. 8524 (1924).

[39] See his account in his autobiography, *Yankee from the West*, chap. 11: "Roxy and the 'Ohio Gang' " (1962).

client, Gordon Campbell, in eighteen cases before Montana courts. Although Wheeler had not appeared as counsel in the court proceedings, was the statute applicable because of his continuing association with his law firm? Also, Wheeler had acted in behalf of Campbell in approaching the Department of the Interior about oil and gas leases. Did this fall within the meaning of the statute, or was it to be construed as a normal responsibility of an elected representative to a constituent?

Only the political issue was effectively resolved in this case; instead of Attorney General Daugherty "getting" Senator Wheeler, the reverse was true. After several weeks of investigation by a Senate committee, President Coolidge obtained Daugherty's resignation. The Senate exonerated Wheeler, and the following year (1925) the federal court found him not guilty of the statutory charge.

In April 1924, a select committee had been appointed by the Senate to investigate Wheeler, after his indictment was voted by the grand jury. Although this committee, under Senator Borah, a Republican from Idaho, exonerated Wheeler of the charges that he had violated a law of the United States, one of its members, Senator Sterling of South Dakota, held a different position. Sterling's minority report dealt largely with the indictment and with evidence that Wheeler had contacted the Department of the Interior on Campbell's behalf. But by an overwhelming vote of 56 to 5, the Senate adopted the majority recommendation.

Because the Senate investigated Wheeler while his trial in a federal court was pending, there might well have been a question —as Sterling pointed out—about the propriety of the Senate's acting while the case was before another branch of the government. The Senate's decision may have decisively affected the judgment of the jurors in Montana, who rendered their verdict almost a year after the Senate exonerated the defendant in their case.

Several cases that commanded the attention of the House in 1924 were somewhat similar to Wheeler's. A United States grand jury in Chicago, investigating charges of fraud in the Veterans Bureau, reported evidence "involving the payment of sums of money to two members of Congress." Because of this report and uncertainty about the identity of the two members, the House requested that additional information be provided by the Attorney General. But Attorney General Daugherty replied that he was reluctant to make the names and the evidence available to the House:

To have two tribunals attempting to act upon the same facts and to hear the same witnesses at the same time will result in confusion and embarrassment and will defeat the ends of justice.[40]

If, however, the House insisted upon receiving this information in exercising its power over its members, Daugherty stated, he would comply. And in such event, he said, he would postpone the action by the Department of Justice until a later date.

Although the House did not want to interfere with the department, it did not want the rumors to continue, inasmuch as they cast a shadow over its entire membership. Then, only a few days after the story had been given to the public, Representatives F. N. Zihlman of Maryland and John Wesley Langley of Kentucky were identified as the implicated congressmen. On March 12, 1924, a select House committee was established to investigate the charges against these two members.

On May 15 the committee submitted its reports and recommendations. Because the evidence had been conflicting and contradictory and the credibility of some of the witnesses had been in doubt, the committee's findings did not "establish the truth of the charge against Representative Zihlman." Therefore, "no further action is required or should be taken by the House."[41] Although the committee also recommended that no further action be taken against Langley, it did so because Langley had already been convicted.

Even though the Attorney General had delayed his investigation, events moved with such rapidity that Langley had been indicted, tried, convicted, and sentenced, and his appeal was pending, by the time the committee reported. And despite the fact that Langley had been found guilty in a court of law, the House displayed a leniency that it had not granted in Berger's case several years earlier. Langley, who in March (when the story first broke) told his applauding colleagues that his thirty years of public service were an open book, seemed to be beyond

---

[40] 65 *Congressional Record* 3803 (1924).
[41] The committees report is in ibid. (May 15, 1924).

reproach. They took no action—not even to declare his seat vacant.

The confusion of the Langley case was compounded later in 1924, and again in December 1925 when the new Congress met. Apparently Langley's constituents also regarded his conduct as unimpeachable, for they had reelected him to Congress in November 1924—after he had been convicted of wrongdoing. And his appeal was still pending on December 9, 1925, when a select committee was created to determine whether he was eligible for membership. Several weeks later, this committee reported that his appeal was still pending; it also stated its belief that the House had no right to punish a member for an offense committed prior to his election. Although the committee acknowledged the problem created by Langley's conviction and the principle that "the House could not permit in its membership a person serving a sentence," it made much of the pending appeal and a promise Langley had made. Langley was not participating in the affairs of Congress, the committee stated, and he had agreed to resign if his appeal was denied. When, on January 11, 1926, his appeal was denied, Langley resigned from a public office to which he had not been sworn.[42]

For various reasons, the recommendations in the committee report were of a doubtful character; nor were these doubts removed by the fact that the House accepted the committee's recommendations. On similar occasions, dating back to the post–Civil War period, it had taken action against members-elect and punished them for prior offenses. Inasmuch as the House, and the Senate as well, had denied membership to men who had been charged with misconduct before their election, was the decision in the Langley case a repudiation of this practice? Both the Bilbo (1947) and the Powell (1967) cases suggest that the earlier precedents were not rejected. Nor is there a consistent rationale for the different treatment of Berger and Langley. In short, different standards were employed between 1919, when Berger was first denied membership, and 1924, when Langley was convicted in a court of law. Many of Berger's "judges" were still in Congress when the House leaned over

---

[42] Matters relating to the Langley case are found in 67 ibid. 1342, 1861 (1925). His wife, Katherine G. Langley, who was elected to succeed him, served four years in the office previously held by her husband.

backward so as not to punish, nor even censure, Langley for misconduct.

The Langley case was only the first of several that cast doubt on the doctrines defined in the Langley committee's reports and underscored how arbitrarily the power to judge could be exercised. The point warrants repetition: the House gave every consideration to Langley while his appeal was pending, yet at other times punished men whose guilt had not been established by due process in a court of law. If, constitutionally, the House could not act against Langley in 1925 because his offenses were committed prior to his reelection, how could the Senate have sat in judgment on Gould and Langer, and how could the Senate justify the exclusion of Bilbo and the House the exclusion of Adam Clayton Powell? Nevertheless, the disposition of three other cases between 1925 and 1967 also seemed to suggest that the Langley case established a new precedent and marked a break with past practices.

The first of these cases occurred in 1933, when an attempt was made to exclude Representative-elect Francis N. Shoemaker of Minnesota because he had once been convicted of sending defamatory material through the mail. However, the House found that Shoemaker met the minimal qualifications prescribed in the Constitution: and it decided that he could not be denied membership by reason of this conviction.[43]

Later, on two occasions in the 1950s, the House was equally lenient, and took no action against two colleagues who had been sentenced to terms in federal penitentiaries. Both men were veteran members of the House—as was Adam Clayton Powell— and both were charged with offenses that were similar to the one later brought against Powell: receiving salary "kickbacks" from non-working persons on the payroll of his congressional staff.

Representative J. Parnell Thomas, who was chairman of the House Committee on Un-American Activities in the Eightieth Congress (1947–1949), was charged with defrauding the government of the United States by taking such kickbacks and, after considerable delay, was brought to trial on November 28, 1949. Almost as soon as his trial began, Thomas pleaded no contest and threw himself on the mercy of the court. On December 2 the *New*

---

43 77 ibid., 73–74, 131–139 (1933).

York Times reported that Thomas's Republican colleagues in Congress were pressuring him to resign, but not until December 10, after he had been sentenced, did Thomas announce that he had submitted his resignation—effective January 2, 1950. Apparently it was appropriate that so vigorous an anti-Communist remain in Congress for another three weeks, his conviction notwithstanding. Evidently his record also justified a deferential restraint: neither at the time of his indictment nor his conviction was there even a hint of House action against him. Moreover, Thomas chose the moment of his retirement from the House— but not, of course, the day on which his prison sentence began.

Several years later, in 1954 and 1955, Representative Ernest K. Bramblett was indicted and convicted for falsifying the payroll record of his staff in collecting kickbacks, and again the House of Representatives deferred all action in favor of the courts.

The Thomas and Bramblett cases arose at a time when Adam Clayton Powell also was a member of the House; indeed, many of the congressmen who passed judgment upon him in 1967, had been in the "silent majority" in the 1950 cases. In 1967, spurning various requests that it choose the same course of inaction it had followed in the former cases, the House chose to act on a political truism restated by Senator Robert Taft of Ohio in 1947 when Theodore Bilbo was denied the oath of office. "You can stop him at the door," declared Taft. "All you need are the votes."[44]

"Stop Him at the Door"

On several occasions congressmen who were intent upon excluding a member-elect would read a verse that supposedly had its origin in a House of Commons exclusion case:

> I hear a lion in the lobby roar! Say, Mr. Speaker,
> Shall we shut the door and keep him out,
> Or shall we let him in
> And see if we can get him out again?

In the Bilbo and Powell cases the answer was obvious: Shut the door and keep them out. Thus, a white supremacist and a black

---

[44] Taft made this statement to newsmen, after which Senator Ellender of Louisiana said it was an immoral statement (93 ibid. 76 [1947]).

militant were denied membership by their respective chambers.

Each man was a veteran member of Congress. Each was charged with misconduct before his election. But neither had been indicted and convicted, unlike Langley, Shoemaker, Thomas, and Bramblett.[45] In both instances, however, race issues and public notoriety were important factors. By treating the white supremacist in the same way they had treated the black militant, congressmen might claim that they were making no distinctions because of race. However, in excluding Bilbo and Powell they could hardly claim that they were acting as they had on other occasions after the exclusion of Berger in 1919 and 1920.

Theodore Bilbo of Mississippi, who was reelected to the Senate in 1946, was accused by other senators of having waged a racist campaign in his bid for reelection and of having used his office and position to obtain gifts from contractors during World War II, and when he presented his credentials in January 1947, a Republican–Northern Democratic coalition prevented his being sworn. However, debate on his exclusion was curtailed when Bilbo underwent surgery for cancer. It was understood that the debate over his eligibility would be resumed after his release from the hospital, but Bilbo died in August 1947 and the Senate let the issue lapse. Whether the Democratic-Republican coalition would have prevailed is wholly problematical, and therefore the only definitive instance in which a member-elect was denied the oath of office after 1920 is the Powell case of 1967.

In the mid-1960s, Adam Clayton Powell's identification with a militant civil rights position did not endear him to his congressional colleagues or to large sections of American society, and least of all his promptings that black communities should practice civil disobedience. "You need not obey laws enacted in political forums wherein you are not represented," he told black audiences. Of parallel significance is the fact that another exclusion case of the 1960s involved Julian Bond, a member of the increasingly militant Student Nonviolent Coordinating Committee (*SNCC*). The exclusion of Julian Bond from the Georgia

---

[45] Indeed, in December 1968 the Department of Justice reported that the evidence did not warrant Powell's criminal prosecution for the misuse of public funds (*New York Times*, Dec. 10, 1968).

House of Representatives and of Adam Clayton Powell from Congress therefore smacked of racial bias.

In neither case was race made the specific issue; the fact that other blacks were seated in both the Georgia legislature and the United States House of Representatives suggested mere coincidence. Nevertheless, a coincidence in which two black men were denied the oath of office to which both had been elected could not be easily accepted within black communities. Even more suspicious, as far as black Americans were concerned, was the different treatment accorded Powell and Senator Thomas Dodd of Connecticut; the offenses for which each man was charged by Congress (but never by a grand jury) seemed equally serious. Because of the race factor, 80 percent of the Negroes polled by Louis Harris in April 1967 believed the white senator would not be as severely punished as the black representative. This belief seemed borne out when the Senate censured Dodd but did not attempt to expel him. Many persons in both the black and the white community believed the Powell and the Dodd cases had been judged by different standards. Typical of this attitude was a political cartoon that pictured Dodd sitting at the front of a bus and Powell sitting in the Jim Crow section at the rear.

Events had been building to a climax for several years. The press had frequently pictured Powell as a playboy-congressman who spent considerable time in the night spots of European capitals. Powell, in turn, told his constituents that the whites were angry because a black congressman was doing openly what white congressmen did surreptitiously. Although it is doubtful that the poverty-stricken inhabitants of the black ghettos received much vicarious satisfaction from Powell's high-level living, they rushed to his support when it looked as if he was to be punished for doing no worse than his privileged white colleagues.

Many of Powell's white colleagues must have felt more than a little uncomfortable as the stories about his foreign junkets at public expense unfolded. Indeed, although some were outraged, others must have felt threatened by Powell's openness and his assertions that his official life style was no different from that of other congressmen. Then, during the debates, one representative said that Powell had been photographed at Bimini with a drink in one hand and a girl in the other—as newsmagazines and newspapers throughout the country attested. Moreover, Washington columnists Drew Pearson and Jack Anderson kept the public informed of congressmen's trips throughout the world at the taxpayers' expense. For one of them to be photographed on a junket that seemed in no way justified was tantamount to a criminal act against Congress that demanded punishment.

As in the case of Whittemore in 1870, the two polygamists and the Mormon elder Cannon (1882), Roberts (1900), and Smoot (1904), and Bilbo in 1947, press coverage and public outrage were probably the most important reasons why Powell was singled out by his colleagues. Besides his openness, he had given the House other reasons for concern. A contempt citation, handed down in a New York court for his failure to pay a judgment in a slander suit was still outstanding. There were his well-publicized trips at government expense, for which there seemed to be no official justification. And there was the payment of a handsome salary to his estranged wife, who resided in Puerto Rico and did not receive the monthly checks. In her appearance before the Select Committee, she reported that she had received only two salary checks, one in November and another in December 1966—when the first investigation of Powell was under way and it was evident that the House would try to exclude him. Nor could she be certain about the recipients of the salary checks that were payable to her between 1961 and November 1966.[46]

The last item—if no other—placed Powell's case in the same category as Thomas's and Bramblett's, but the Department of Justice report of December 1968, that the evidence did not warrent criminal prosecution, seemed to extend more leniency to Powell than had been granted to the other two men. This report, therefore, could have been motivated by reasons other than insufficient evidence, in view of the outcry that the case against Powell was motivated by racism. Also, Powell's reelection in a special election in April 1967 and in the regular election of November 1968 showed that he had overwhelming approval among black voters regardless of what the "white power struc-

---

[46] From testimony of Yvette Diago Powell before the Select Committee on Feb. 16, 1967 (*In re Adam Clayton Powell: Hearings pursuant to H. Res. 1*, 90th Congress, 1st sess., p. 204 [1967]). The committee investigated the New York contempt citation, the frequent and apparently unjustified trips abroad taken by Powell and his staff, and the salary matter (ibid., passim).

ture" thought of him, and because racism and racial incidents had inflamed so many black communities, it seemed unwise for public officials to aggravate the situation. Finally, by late 1968 many officials in Washington would not have been unhappy if the whole matter would simply disappear. Although some representatives were still intent upon punishing Powell, most of them—including the House leaders in both parties—were trying to pour oil on the troubled waters.

Powell's reelection in November 1968 produced a new and crucial attitude among many of his antagonists and protagonists. Uncertain about the Supreme Court's response to his appeal but confronted with still another overwhelming vote of approval from Powell's black constituents, the House leaders did not want a replay of the 1967 exclusion incident. Therefore the actions the Select Committee proposed in 1967 and the House followed in 1969 leave us as uncertain today as at any other time in our history about the extent and nature of a chamber's power to judge its members.

In 1967 the Select Committee reported that, in deciding whether Powell was eligible for membership, the House could consider only the age, citizenship, and inhabitancy requirements of the Constitution. However, it suggested that the House punish Powell by imposing a fine of $40,000.[47] In effect, therefore, the committee answered the time question by saying that the House can judge past conduct in exercising its power over its members.

But this is not a real answer. It conforms neither with the Langley and Shoemaker decisions nor the general tenor of the committee's recommendations. If Powell could not be judged on grounds other than age, citizenship, and inhabitancy, how could the House punish him by imposing a fine? If Powell had commit-

---

[47] My examination of the cases leads to the conclusion that this was the first time a fine had been recommended. It seems evident that the purpose was to punish Powell and thus satisfy his critics with a penalty less severe than exclusion. Obviously this course of action did not succeed. However, the committee's recommendation did serve as a precedent and in January 1969, when the House voted to seat Powell, a $25,000 fine was imposed. Because a fixed amount was withheld from his paycheck each month to pay this fine, Representative Powell described himself as a part-time congressman. His attendance record had not been exemplary in the past. Now he felt justified in spending most of his time away from Washington.

ted offenses that warranted a severe punishment, these offenses must have warranted criminal prosecution. Yet in December 1968 the Department of Justice reported there were insufficient grounds for seeking an indictment.

Nevertheless, the House was still committed to obtaining some kind of satisfaction. Already punished by having been deprived of a veteran congressman's prerogative of inestimable value, seniority, Powell was subjected to another penalty, a $25,000 fine. The latter was imposed in January 1969, when Powell was given the oath of office.

Powell might have won vindication in 1969 when the Supreme Court declared his exclusion unconstitutional. However, since this ruling was, at best, an inadequate answer to the various questions, and did not result in Powell's recovery of his back salary, seniority, and $25,000 fine, it may prove to be meaningless. Whether Representative Powell will say with Pyrrhus "One more such victory and I am lost" depends not so much on the Supreme Court as upon each chamber's realization of the way in which its exercise of power affects democracy.

VII

Implications for Democracy of
Congress's Quasi-Judicial Power

No matter what inferences were drawn immediately after the Supreme Court's declaration in June 1969 that the House had exceeded its constitutional authority in denying membership to Powell, it soon became evident that its decision was unenforceable. The weakness and the inadequacy of that decision (discussed in Chapter 1) were sufficient reasons for questioning whether *Powell* v. *McCormack* (1969) meant a repudiation of past practices and a safeguarding of democratic principles for the future.

Obviously, Representative Powell thought the decision was a significant victory for him and for democracy, for he heralded *Powell* v. *McCormack* as confirming his faith in the American political system. But it soon became obvious that the House would not accept the Court's decision. Told that it had exceeded its constitutional authority, it did not try to correct its error by restoring Powell's $25,000 fine and congressional seniority. There was little fanfare, and scarcely any bombast, when the *Powell* decision was announced, but a more or less silent House of Representatives was not a subdued or compliant House. Instead of agreeing with the Court about the extent of a chamber's power to judge the qualifications of its members and recompensing Powell, it prepared for further litigation, and therefore confrontation, in and with the federal courts.

An even greater weakness of the *Powell* decision was the failure of the Court in February 1970 to confirm its decision that Powell was entitled to recover both the fine and his seniority. In June 1969, in self-assured manner, it had pronounced that a judicial remedy was available, but in less than a year it was apparent that the Court was convinced of its limitations. Although it could declare that the House had exceeded its constitutional authority, it could not provide Powell the judicial remedy that would have made its first *Powell* decision meaningful.

Thus *Powell* v. *McCormack* was an abortive incident in a 180-year history rather than a redefinition of the dimensions of a particular congressional power. Adam Clayton Powell enjoyed a brief period of illusory victory; but Congress had not changed. Each house would still define its own powers and exercise its authority to judge its members as it saw fit. The most we can say is that *Powell* v. *McCormack* focused national attention on the arbitrariness with which a chamber can exercise its power over its members and members-elect.

The problem of self-administered powers that can be exercised in arbitrary and inconsistent ways is directly traceable to the Constitution, which authorizes both chambers to judge the elections, returns, qualifications, and conduct of their members. These powers are conferred in vague language, and with only one exception are not subject to specified restraints (a two-thirds vote is required for expelling a member). These powers are neither specific in their meaning nor fully defined in their scope. For example, there are no constitutional specifics on when a member-elect must have met the minimal requirements so as to be eligible for membership or when and where a member's offense must have occurred to be within the jurisdiction of a house.

Some Americans—such as Professor Charles Warren and various members of Congress and federal judges—have argued that the limitations on these powers are to be found in the intent of the delegates to the Constitutional Convention, in their resolution of various issues, and in the comments of Madison and Hamilton in *The Federalist*. However, as was argued in Chapter 2, Professor Warren's thesis and the claims of others cannot support the weight of other evidence.

For example, the argument that the convention intended to restrict the judicial power of Congress to the three qualifications of age, citizenship, and inhabitancy fails to acknowledge other prescriptions in the Constitution: the four disqualifications in the original text and the disability provision in the Fourteenth Amendment. Nor can we agree with Professor Warren that neither chamber "should possess a power which the Convention had refused to vest in the whole Congress"—that neither chamber can devise additional tests of fitness and Congress cannot use its legislative power to prescribe additional qualifications for membership. Such a conclusion is undermined by the provision of Article VI that forbids a religious test as a condition for holding office and the action of the First Congress in providing an additional disqualification by statute.

The situation is clear. *Powell* v. *McCormack* did not affect the power of either chamber in any manner; therefore the House and the Senate can exercise their respective powers in the same arbitrary and capricious manner that typifies the hundred-year period before Powell was excluded from office. They can also, therefore, continue to temporize the two democratic principles of power subject to external checks and the right of the people to choose their own representative. Since their power to judge is only self-restrained and can be exercised at the whim of a congressional majority, democracy suffers. And since this power is exclusive in and subject to arbitrary exercise by a legislative chamber, the right of the people to choose the men who will represent them is negatively affected.

At the very least, there must be grave doubt that any power of a democracy should be beyond the reach of externally applied restraints. The history of Congress in judging the qualifications and conduct of its members demonstrates what can happen when power is not subject to restraints. We have but to recall the different standards applied by the House to Berger in 1919 and 1920, to Langley in 1924 and 1925, to Shoemaker in 1933, to Thomas in 1949 and 1950, to Bramblett in 1954 and 1955, and to Powell in 1967–1969 to realize that unrestrained or only self-restrained power can be arbitrarily exercised. Serious differences in standards, nonuniformity in action, and general inconsistencies are much too obvious to be dismissed. Their consequences for democracy are much too great to warrant dismissal.

Because it is not possible for an external agency, not even the people within a constituency, to impose restraints upon the power of either chamber, Congress itself must be concerned about reform. As the Supreme Court noted in *Powell* v. *McCormack*, from the time of Reconstruction to

the present, Congressional practice has been erratic; and on the few occasions when a member-elect was excluded although he met all the qualifications set forth in the Constitution, there were frequently vigorous dissents.

Inasmuch as Roberts, Berger, and Powell were punished by exclusion, whereas the House scarcely noted the serious acts of misconduct committed by Langley, Shoemaker, Thomas, and Bramblett, dissent and criticism are inevitable. As long as Powell could be severely punished, while Dodd, whose alleged offenses were equally serious, was only censured, there would be many Americans who must protest the application of different standards.

Neither chamber can overlook these inconsistencies or disregard their motivation. If meaningful reform is to be introduced, both houses must use their collective legislative power in attacking the central problem. Congress should introduce uniform standards. Just as on other occasions Congress has prescribed statutory disqualifications, it can enact comprehensive legislation to achieve uniformity in standards of qualification.

Rather than belabor the questions about the nature and scope of congressional power and the intent of the Founding Fathers, Congress should proceed on the assumption that it can judge a man's fitness on grounds other than those prescribed in the Constitution. If Congress continues to act on the same uncertain grounds as it has in the past, it must expect still other instances in which different standards will be employed; and democracy must suffer. On the other hand, if Congress were to agree that the implied authorization in the provision that prohibits a religious test and the statutory disqualification in the 1790 act are a firm basis for its claim to a broad power, it could proceed toward effecting a meaningful reform. By removing doubts about a chamber's broad power and asserting that each chamber has such a power (which has a sound basis in historical evidence), Congress could move resolutely toward safeguarding vital democratic principles. The alternative is to continue to operate in the shadows of doubt and uncertainty.

Only if there is standardization can Congress solve the principal problem in keeping with democratic goals. And standardization can be achieved only through legislation. In enacting a law that stipulates the grounds for disqualification, Congress can call upon many precedents. So many different kinds of offenses have been charged against members of Congress—treasonous conduct, bribery, polygamy, misuse of the powers of office, payroll padding, salary kickbacks, and defrauding the government of the United States—that Congress has but to look to earlier cases to define grounds in statute for a man's being disqualified for membership.

However, Congress would have to look to matters other than qualifications and disqualifications. In enacting a comprehensive statute it would have to decide, for example, whether mere suspicion of guilt is enough to warrant action against a member. There have been a number of occasions on which a member has been punished even though his guilt was not established in a court of law. In 1807 Senator John Smith of Ohio was the object of an expulsion move despite the fact that he was not tried—as the Senate's charge implied he should be—as a co-conspirator of Aaron Burr. Similarly, Adam Clayton Powell was punished in 1967 and again in 1969 although the Department of Justice reported that the evidence against him did not justify a proceeding before a federal grand jury. Congress has but to compare many widely separated cases—for example, those of Langley, Thomas, and Bramblett—to note their differences in action and standards and, therefore, the reasons for their inconsistent outcomes. It would therefore seem proper that this legislation provide that guilt as established in accord with regularly established judicial procedures, rather than mere suspicion, be the grounds for declaring a man unfit to serve in Congress.

Finally, to achieve standardization Congress will have to answer the time and place questions. The Shoemaker, Gould, Langer, Bilbo, and Powell cases are some of the twentieth-century cases that suggest the necessity of definitive answers. As long as any doubt persists about the relationship of the time and place questions to Congress's power to judge qualifications or conduct, jurisdictional uncertainty will persist and different standards will be employed.

By defining the nature and the scope of its powers in statute, Congress will not only introduce standardization but will safeguard democratic principles that it has often ignored or inadvertently undermined in the past.

Index

167